CW00969023

TOUR THE CORE

THE PATHWAY TO A POSITIVELY JOYOUS LIFE

BY

THERESA BORG

Copyright © 2015 THERESA BORG

All rights reserved. No part of this book may be used or
reproduced in any manner whatsoever without written
permission of the author except for the 'fair use' of brief
quotations embodied in critical articles or reviews. For further
information contact the author at:

HTTP://WWW.POSITIVELYJOYOUS.COM

The information presented in this book should not be
considered or treated as a substitute for professional medical or
mental health advice: always consult a medical practitioner.
Any use of the strategies and information in this book is at the
reader's discretion and risk. The author cannot be held
responsible for any loss, claim or damage arising from the use,
misuse or suggestions made.

The moral rights of the author have been asserted.

Contents

Introduction

"You are not your body or your mind. Your body and mind – actually the whole world exists in you." Deepak Chopra

Isn't life great?

Isn't the gift of being alive positively joyous?

When I was young, my extended family and I used to go on trips to the countryside every Sunday. At the end of the day, the uncles would put the tiny ones in a big blanket and pick up the corners to make a huge hammock-like swing for us all. I still remember looking forward to that moment with such glee, laughing and enjoying the excitement of it all. Life was so simple then.

Can you remember a time when everything was fun and you were constantly laughing? When was the last time that you felt *that* good? More to the point perhaps, when was the last time that you actually *allowed* yourself to feel that good?

It is so easy to forget how precious life is. Most of us love life so much that, if we were to be given a terminal prognosis, we would fight tooth and nail to survive. So I want you to remember every day how absolutely fabulous life is. I want to help you to *remind yourself* that life is meant to be positively joyous. I will do this by giving you the simple tools that I have found helpful in my own life and in my work as a coach, meditation teacher and hypnotherapist.

This book is a straightforward guide to happiness and self-empowerment via the removal of bugs and virus programs from the belief systems of your mind.

As I will explain going forward, I believe that we exist in a physical environment solely to enable us to interact with other people and things. It is through these interactions that we come to know and understand who we really are on the deepest levels. We exist in relation to everyone and everything else around us. As a consequence, everyone and everything around us become the mirrors and tools that we use for our own learning and growth.

It is our beliefs and perceptions about these relationships that we use to create our "reality". We must, therefore, pay close attention to the nature of all of our thoughts and beliefs. If we create our own "reality", then we must also take full responsibility for everything that we create. So it really matters what we think and to what we direct our attention.

Our power and responsibility for creation are total. Indeed, each one of us is the writer, the director and producer of the glorious 'play' that is our life. In this book I will show how you can take full responsibility for your creation and thereby let go of the idea of victimhood forever. If you are experiencing any problems in your life then you are also capable of creating the solutions. I will argue that this is the most empowering way to live your life.

I chose the title Tour the Core to reflect my journey from deep depression to amazing bliss, by using both the CORE and TOUR strategies for happiness. A tour guide must know the route, the highlights and points of interest. Your guide must know the history and facts about those places of interest and be able to answer all of your questions. I believe that I have both the personal, professional experience and indeed qualifications to be that guide.

CORE is an easy to remember acronym that stands for Confidence, Opinion, Rightness and Excitement. I have created this simple and yet effective strategy to facilitate everyday awareness of what is going on around you and how to constantly use that awareness for your own benefit.

TOUR is an acronym for a process of work I have designed to help you uncover, change and release troublesome belief programs.

This book is unique because it provides worksheets for the TOUR and supporting meditation tools which are available within the book or as downloads from my website http://www.positivelyjoyous.com

You are a complex, layered physical being. If you really want to create change in your life and to release the old patterns and stuck energy, then you need to clear them on all levels of body, mind and spirit. Therefore with a fully holistic approach in mind, I will draw together ideas from mainstream psychology, the law of attraction, spirituality, mindfulness and Buddhism. These terms and sources will all be explained later.

I will also argue that you are a powerful, spiritual consciousness within a physical body, experiencing being human. Our true essence is a triad that includes Spirit – You (and) and All That Is. You are Spiritual.

With that in mind, I ask that you make yourself important, valuable and absolutely happy before anything else. This is not being selfish. What I am actually promoting is the quality that I will differentiate as 'self-is-ness'.

'Self-is-ness' is the honouring of who and what you are: the amazing creation of the universe. It is achieved by asking and seeking happiness for the self, first, knowing what you want and accepting that you deserve to have it because you are simply following your normal, natural instincts! Being able to keep your own 'cup' full of joy and love will enable you make a real difference to the world. We can influence and inspire others simply by our example. It is not necessarily what you do in life that is valuable but who you really are. 'You matter' is the incredibly powerful and positive declaration that you are a creator: important, deserving and that you love yourself.

You are unique, you are special and you will only be *this you* once in eternity so it is important to make it count. I want to help you to value every single moment of your life because you will never get that moment again.

To be self-reflective and self-aware allows you to come to know and accept yourself fully on all levels. If you do not own everything that is happening to you, how can you be in a position to change it? You will forever be a victim to the peaks and troughs of life. If you are the problem then you too are the solution and that is really taking your power back! There are amazing rewards that can be gleaned from a mere willingness to change.

Everything that happens is a choice, your choice, your creation – the good, the bad and the ugly. I want to make sure that you always choose the best because you deserve it. Life can be much simpler than we make it. Nothing is too good to be true if you allow that to become your program or belief of choice.

I pulled myself out of a dark night of the Soul with all of these processes and tools. I only teach those strategies that I have found and used successfully to engender powerful and positive change in my life. I believe that the resulting joy was my gift from the Universe and I now pass this gift on to you.

So are you now ready to create the life that you desire and deserve? If so, dear friends, climb aboard for the TOUR and do not forget to enjoy the ride!

Chapter 1: Who Are You?

"The unexamined life is not worth living." Socrates

Have you ever sat down and really contemplated why you are here and where you have come from? It seems to me that to *not* ask these questions is in some ways to miss the point of life itself.

If we don't ask ourselves those questions, we often end up in a state of limbo, merely existing rather than living the full technicolour, glorious experience of life. It took me many years during a long bout of depression to wake up to the fact that I was not living but just 'existing'. My soul or spirit was dying.

I was desperately unhappy.

To be honest, at that point I had never sat down and taken the time to think about what happiness really meant to me. But I now wholeheartedly agree with the Greek philosopher Aristotle who said: "Happiness is the meaning and the purpose of life, the whole aim and end of human existence".

Today, I often ask depressed clients what their passion is. "Erm…" is normally the reply. I say to them: 'blue-sky thinking, what would you love your day to look like?' (Blue-sky thinking means there are no limits of time, money, ability etc.) "Erm ..." is normally the reply. Why are you here? What is your purpose? "Erm ..." You get the picture, I think.

So how can you get to a place of happiness, fulfilment and excitement if you have never even thought about what that looks like? How can you even start to move in that direction? It is like saying you want to go on holiday, not doing anything about it, and then complaining because everyone else is on holiday.

It amuses me to imagine God standing with the gift box of possibilities, eager to distribute the goodies, but completely frustrated as he waits for us to decide what it is we really want! We will see later that there is a law of the universe which states that when you ask for anything with focused thought it is immediately given. But to get what you really want, you do have to ask for it first!

So what is this elusive concept called happiness? According to the dictionary, happiness is:
1. The quality or state of being happy. (Great, this tells us nothing!)
2. Good fortune; pleasure; contentment; joy.

Happiness, I find, is like love in many ways. It is an ephemeral quality that we want so much but which is incredibly difficult to define. Ultimately, happiness is simply an emotional state of being, and our emotions, as we shall see, can be totally under our control.

Often though, we become locked into the belief system that our happiness can only come from other 'things' or other people. Sadly, that belief program will *always* keep us as a victim in life. If that person or 'thing' fails to manifest or live up to our expectations then we become sad or depressed. Waiting for happiness to appear in some external form often causes us to put our lives on hold until that nebulous date when 'the thing' or 'the one' shows up. We unconsciously say to ourselves, "I will accept existing like this until I get the 'thing' I want and then I will be happy and I will really live".

That is conditional living.

In some ways, this is what we do in romantic relationships and friendships. We demand that the other person behaves in ways that make us happy and we thus end up living conditional love: I can only be happy or love you if you fulfil the conditions that will make me happy!

Breaking news: No-one was put on this earth to make you happy! It is your responsibility to make yourself happy. Happiness is not a 'thing'.

Buddha said, "There is no way to happiness, happiness is the way".

Obtaining true and lasting happiness which can never be threatened is a state that you achieve internally first. The only way to happiness is to know, understand and take full ownership of who you really are. That means self-acceptance — warts and all. Exploration of the self through experience is ultimately then the essence of our existence.

Take a moment and think of the happiest person you know. Think about *why* that person is so happy. This is a really good exercise because so often we feel so far removed from happiness that we just cannot reach it within ourselves. Therefore to 'model' others is a valuable tool.

Often the reason you are drawn to this person is because they are actually a reflection of your current vibrational state or the treasure that is hidden within you. I will explore in more detail later my theory that everyone in our lives is a mirror to our hidden traits and treasures.

I believe that happiness is our natural state. The question that follows then is: why is it so difficult to access and maintain that state?

Well, the shocking answer is that bliss is boring! At least it becomes so after a while.

When I met my husband we both loved eating out. We ate in a different restaurant every Saturday night for a year or so. By the end of that year, we were both so bored of eating out that it was no longer a pleasure. Eating out had become routine.

As humans, we are programmed to constantly grow and to evolve. We cannot get anywhere from by remaining still. We have to move position in order to get a better view. We develop from being exposed to contrast and change. We need challenges, both negative and positive.

Thus, whenever we ask for something external to bring us happiness, the problem is that the novelty of that 'thing' will wear off pretty quickly. We then look for the next car, the next exciting encounter or the next house. For me, once I have received the thing that I have asked for, there is an incredibly short time before I am thinking about my next request and rightly so.

This is a crucial point. We are programmed to search out excitement, challenge and growth! The problem is that we do not recognise that this is a normal and natural state and instead view change as negative. We ask ourselves: Why doesn't our happiness ever last? What are we doing wrong? Why does it always go wrong for me?

We even have sayings (belief programs) such as, "All good things come to an end." We often assume that the ending of the 'pleasant thing' is necessarily a negative occurrence. As we shall see, everything in life is perception and judgement or, in other words, *how you choose* to see things. If instead, we accept that change is constant, inevitable and beneficial then we free ourselves from the fear of it! If our natural drive was not to move and improve, life would never have got past the point of being a single-celled amoeba. It is not greedy to want more, to be more or to have more; these are natural drives and as such they should be honoured.

Pause for a moment and think about all the beliefs about greed you have acquired or collected over the years. Are these beliefs correct? If so, where is the evidence that they are true? Who gets to decide what is right or wrong? Is it not possible to want more and to be personally responsible enough to achieve these desires without negatively affecting anyone else? Most of us have a fully-functioning moral compass after all.

I am not advocating taking anything from anyone else. There is also no need to do so as the universe is amazingly abundant and miraculous. You do not get well from draining wellness from anyone else. Your good health comes from within you. This is the same with *all* things. If you ask, it is given but you have to then allow whatever you have asked for to manifest. We will learn more about this in the chapter on the Law of Attraction. For now, let's just say that this is why self-is-ness is vital for our happiness.

Knowing what you want and accepting that you deserve to have it is not being selfish. 'Self-is-ness' is the honouring of who and what you are: the amazing creation of the universe. By asking and seeking happiness for the self-first, it could be argued that you are simply following your normal, natural instincts!

We must also recognise that happiness is basically a transitory state. One of the most remarkable principles I have learned from Buddhism is to accept that everything is impermanent and *will* change. In fact, change is actually one of the few things that you can always rely on in life! Acceptance or, better still, the welcoming of change puts an end to suffering very quickly.

Change equals growth and thus must be positive because all personal growth is ultimately positive. Of course, we may judge things as negative in the moment, but that may be just because in that moment we are not seeing the bigger picture. In fact, with hindsight, I am sure most people would agree that their biggest traumas actually turned out to be their greatest lessons. Circumstances which can feel disastrous in that moment often contain the most valuable treasure buried within them.

Everything in life is in a constant state of motion. Even a rock that looks solid is constantly eroding and being transformed. Physicists tell us that we are actually pure energy. And as energy is never static and can never be destroyed, our natural state must therefore be one of constant motion or transformation and growth. Our transformational cycle continuously takes us through physical form to non-physical energy and back again. We recognise this as the cycle of life and death. But although this is the case, we can never fully separate ourselves from being an eternal energy. I call this energy the soul.

Avicenna, a first century philosopher of Arabic origin, performed this thought experiment and proposed:

If I was suspended in mid-air and blindfolded so that I would not know that I had a body, I would still know that I existed.

The soul, Avicenna concluded, 'must be different from the body.'

A soul when in non-physical form is a nebulous, ephemeral energy. I believe this is the real and eternal 'you' that can never be destroyed. The true essence of 'you' is the energy and consciousness that flows through the body and animates the physical vehicle that you are currently occupying.

Just as your computer is incomplete and static without an electricity supply, so your physical body is incomplete and static without your soul essence or *life force*. The real purpose and value of electricity only becomes clear when it is into a localised point of reception like a computer. The computer is unimportant for the existence of the electricity but the computer is vitally important for the expression of the electricity. For my computer, electricity is a vital element for it to have purpose and meaningful existence. Similarly, the soul energy finds purpose, value and meaning as it becomes channelled into a 'physical' body. Life then is the joy of a soul experiencing through the physical senses.

Pause for a moment and notice how much of life is actually made up of sensory experiences.

All of it is! So why would the soul want this experience?

Imagine for a moment All That Is or God is the only thing that exists. It would have all the knowledge of everything included within it. However, this is knowledge or information, but not experience. It is the difference between reading lots of books about Egypt at home or essentially visiting Egypt. You now know through *sensory experience* that which you merely knew as information before. Which offers the richest and fullest knowledge? Would you prefer reading about the magnificent Egyptian pyramids or seeing, smelling, touching and having the grand experience of them in person? The purpose of life is simply in the joy of experiencing it sensually and this, of course, is also the fun of the journey!

Personally, I do not think that any form of human existence has to have a grand intent or purpose as judged by academic or perhaps professional achievements. I believe that everything that we are, do and achieve is in itself a beautiful gift to and from the universe.

We get to choose who to be, what to do and have, and it is all good. It all adds to the experience of existence. Existence is because existence just loves to be. Everything that we do, then, could be said to be valid as a human being.

Several years ago, I wrote a eulogy for my granddad that struck a chord with a lot of people. I did not write it with any great philosophical intent at the time, but just as a mere reflection of how I saw his life.

My grandfather was a wonderful though very quiet and unassuming man who was well loved and respected. He worked hard all his life and raised his family quietly. He never climbed Mount Everest, walked on the moon nor won a Nobel Prize. Still to this day however, many years on, wherever I go locally, people remember him and the kindness that he always showed to others.

Who is to judge that my granddad's life was not amazing? Could it be that he changed the world just by being an inspirational example to us all? If a life needs to be measured at all, in my opinion, it should be measured by who you are, not by what you have achieved. Of course, if your life is full of amazing achievements I think that is absolutely wonderful. But if you are just happy being you, I think that is just as magnificent.

Obviously, how you feel about what I have just written will go some way to answering the questions at the beginning of the chapter about why you are here and where you have come from. But remember this — we can't all be great academics because who then would fix the electricity when it breaks down? If you were on a desert island and life was about just finding food, who would you want as your companion — the fisherman or the painter? My point is that we all have our place and we are *all* important; we all are loved, supported by and valuable to the overall growth of the universe.

Creation has afforded us the gift of complete free will and thus the ability to choose exactly what we do or do not do with our lives. Any proposed, predefined purpose or destiny would by its very existence oppose the possibility for free will to exist. The existence of our free will also makes illogical any final judgement by 'God'!

If I left a small child in a white room with coloured crayons and gave him or her complete freedom, how could I then return and berate the child for having drawn on the walls? Free will means just that. You are free to do what you will. Existing in a physical environment of cause and effect however, you will, of course be aware that every action has a consequence.

In some ways, the easiest way to live a happy life is simply to live in the present and to constantly move toward the next thing that will make you feel happy and joyous. Remember that all of nature is naturally programmed to move towards pleasure and away from pain. In fact, it sometimes appears as if humans are the only species that *seeks out* pain and misery rather than following this natural instinct!

The real problem for some of us is that we are making choices unconsciously and so it feels like bad stuff just happens to us. We are sure that we would not deliberately choose the pain, the suffering or the negative experiences that we may be going through.

It is true though that we are so free that we can even choose to experience growth through suffering or ignorance. Any uninvited interference by anyone or anything else immediately nullifies a person's true free will and freedom. Even the Bible reminds us of this fact,

"But God does not overrule a person's free will. Ultimately he will surrender to it and as in the case of Pharaoh even abandon someone to it" Exodus 8:32

My depression, for example, was a terrible thing to live through but actually created the biggest opportunity for growth of my entire life.

It now affords me unique insight into others' suffering and thus the ability to help free them from it.

However, along with the 'right' to free will comes responsibility. We create everything that happens to us — the good, the bad and the ugly and we must take full responsibility for it. The good news is that you can change and 'wake up' to how you are creating those negative experiences.

It is possible to discover the belief programs that create our negative experiences and to remove them from the 'computer.'

Often we need the contrast of what we do not want in order to be able to see clearly what it is that we do want. If this is the case, we have to accept that the negative experiences in our lives need to be there so we can draw out from within them the positive experiences that we do want. This natural process is set up to continuously remind us to keep adjusting our focus towards that which we do want.

Once we achieve a basic level of contentment, we have to keep focused on more things and reasons to feel happy. I believe that positivity is a muscle that needs to be 'worked out' every day. Any good gym instructor will advise you that you have to maintain your regime and increase the resistance against the muscle in order for it to have a training effect and grow. Like anything in life, use it or lose it! Make it your intention every day to remember to go to the happiness gym.

Never allow yourself to become complacent about joy. I now wake up and the first thought that I allow to be in my mind is, 'Thank you for the best day yet!' Opportunities to find that happiness set point are readily available every minute of the day. For example, I love to feel the warmth of the sun, to take in the vibrant colours around me or to enjoy the warm feeling that comes from drinking a cup of tea on a cold winter's day. Remember that the very best things in life are freely given by an abundant universe.

Finally, in honour of you as an interconnected essential part of that universe, allow me to reinforce your true form as an individualised, focused portion of the original 'Source' energy of the universe.

Pause and reflect for a moment on this: if you were to remove all of the labels attached to you, your environment and everything in your environment, what would remain?

Energy! Everything as one! What is! All That Is! God?

Remove the labels and you start to notice that everything is actually all one thing aside from the arbitrary divisions of language. Language, "my body – your body", is the only thing that separates us as individuals if you think about it philosophically. Quantum physics is now discussing ideas of interconnectedness and is supporting what many of the oldest spiritual traditions and religions have always proposed — that we are all one, inextricably connected through an energy field. Once you allow the boundaries to disappear, that sense of separation which influences us so negatively simply melts away.

If we accept this is the case, then spiritually and in some ways physically speaking, you must be as good as everyone else around you because we are all the same. We are literally one thing - energy. I like to think of us as simply 'bags of cells'.

In conclusion then, as reflections of nature which naturally strive towards growth and joy, we too are here to do that. However, we are free to evolve our soul in whatever form that we may choose to do that in. We have free will and choice at every juncture of life.

However, I did say earlier that any uninvited interference by anyone or anything else would immediately nullify a person's free will and freedom. But I propose that you are actually able and entitled to *invite* help and guidance whenever you need it. What's more, that help and guidance will immediately be given. However it may appear in a form that looks nothing like a giant angel with white fluffy wings.

Chapter 2: The Little Voices in Your Head

"The mind is everything and what you think you become."
Buddha

In this chapter I will invite you to consider some evidence and ideas that support my belief that we are so much more than we think we are and thus capable of so much more than we may have previously believed.

So first let us begin to explore a world that is far more mysterious than you may have realised.

A boyfriend and I were once discussing miracles. He stated, quite categorically that he did not believe in them. Then to my astonishment, he went on to recount a story about being in a cabriolet car, losing control on the motorway, overturning several times and walking away without a scratch. I thought to myself …and that wasn't a miracle?!!

I pondered what he would accept as a miracle. Did Jesus or a giant angel have to pluck him out of the car and lower him safely back to ground to the sound of celestial trumpeters in order for it to count as a miracle?

Think about your own life. Maybe you are encountering miracles every day without giving them their true credit. I experienced a minor miracle today. When I arrived home from work, I went into the kitchen to find that the cat had pushed forward the lever on the tap over the sink and the sink was filling with water. As the plug hole was covered, the water was literally just about to run over the top and spill onto the floor when I arrived just in the nick of time to turn it off.

Stop for a moment and think about how you would categorise that incident. Often, we dismiss things as 'lucky'. Change the word lucky to miracle and see how differently you feel about it! If I knew a mathematical genius, I would ask him or her to calculate the odds of all the things that needed to occur synchronously in order for me to arrive home just in time to avert disaster. It would have to include the actions of the cat, the rate of flow of the water, the traffic and so on.

Miraculous, I *choose* to believe.

I have had the good fortune to experience some amazing miracles. For instance, I was staying in the beautiful small Spanish town of Orgiva when my friend, her daughter and I decided to walk back to our villa which was about 30 minutes out of the village via a scenic route. It was about 35 degrees Celsius in the midday sun and we got hopelessly lost. We had been walking for about two hours and there was literally nothing except olive groves. We had run out of water and my friend's daughter became very distressed. In desperation I prayed to God to help us. Literally within two minutes or so, we came out of some trees to find a very big road in front of us. A car stopped and inside was a wonderful English woman. Even more amazingly, she was on her way to her father's villa in the hills, which was just above the villa where we were staying. So not only were we saved, but we were saved by an English woman who took us all the way to our door!

Now that's what I call a miracle!

For me the world holds so much more mystery than we see with the naked eye. Miracles and guidance are manifest around us all the time. More often than not, that help and guidance may appear to be very mundane. It may look like the right book, the right teacher, a strange coincidence or even the words of a song. Most of the time you can access that help and guidance easily and all that is required is to listen to the quiet voice inside your own head.

Whether we are aware of it or not that little voice inside our head is constantly giving us messages and guidance. Whether we choose to listen to them or not is a different matter.

I was recently reading an interesting book by Anthony Peake called The Daemon in which he discusses the Eidolon, which is the Greek term for the lower everyday self, and the Daemon, which in my terminology is akin to the Higher Self.

The Greeks believed that the Daemon is a reflection of the Gods within every Being. Peake proposes that this Daemon inhabits the right side of the brain, has access to the future, and is constantly offering you messages and guidance.

Intrigued by this idea, I asked in my morning meditation to hear my Daemon clearly. Later that morning, as I was collating the student's homework from one of my classes, I heard a loud voice in my head which said:

"The computer is about to switch off and you have not saved your work!"

As I was immersed in my work, I decided to finish the page that I was working on when suddenly, just as the voice had predicted, the computer crashed.

I laughed out loud as I thought to myself, "Wow, that was so clear and I STILL managed to ignore it!"

In a state of shock and some amusement, I intuitively asked if my Higher Self had a name and was 'given' what I clearly heard as Hermione. Later, when I came to write the name down, however, I found myself writing the name Amione. It was only some weeks later that I realised that it spelled -

AM-I-ONE?

Wow!!! My mind was blown by the significance of this name as obviously the voice of my Higher Self was telling me clearly that it is in fact one with me.

The analogy Peake offers about the Daemon is that 'I' sit inside the train and look out of the window on 'my life', I can see a little of the past, the present view and maybe just a sliver of the future. My Daemon Amione, however, rides confidently on the roof of the train and sees where I have come from, the reality of the present as well as the amazing possibilities in my future. She sees the whole picture! This is obviously an invaluable asset to have when making important decisions in our lives.

The Split Brain

Scientific evidence that the brain is split can be found in a wonderful book by Frederick Schiffer called 'Of Two Minds'. In the book, Schiffer discusses the results of a procedure called a commissurotomy that was developed for debilitated temporal lobe epileptics. The aim of the operation was to prevent a seizure spreading from one hemisphere of the brain and thus causing damage to the other. The operation involves the cutting of the Corpus Callosum (the bridge between the two hemispheres). In the book, Schiffer recounts the doctor's amazement as the procedure resulted in the creation, albeit temporarily, of two exact intelligent and autonomous minds. I would like to propose that one of those intelligent minds as exposed by this research is in fact the Higher Self or Daemon.

I would also like to propose that the heart is actually steering our actions via its communication with the Higher Self in the right brain.

This theory is backed up by findings at the American research foundation the Institute of HeartMath (IHM) which discovered that the heart receives information before the brain, processes it and then appears to influence us towards behaviour that is beneficial for the individual. The IHM concluded that the brain is not necessarily the organ through which our decisions are *made*, but instead the tool through which things are *managed*.

The left brain mainly controls the right side of the body and vice versa. It seems to me no coincidence, then, that my heart is on the left side of the body and my Higher Self in the right hemisphere of the brain. I believe that the heart together with my Higher Self is actually responsible for the decisions that I believe I am consciously making.

There is a fascinating experiment which illustrates this point perfectly in a BBC documentary called 'Horizon – The Secret You'.

In the documentary, a professor visits researchers at a hospital in Berlin. He takes part in an experiment whereby he is placed in an MRI scanner which shows in real time the areas of the brain that are illuminated when we think certain thoughts or perform certain actions.

The researchers asked the professor to press either the left or right button on their command. It was up to the professor whether he chose the left or right button. As he pressed the button, the researchers could clearly see which areas of the brain lit up. They showed that when the professor pressed the left button, there was brain activity that lit up in a definite pattern. When the professor pressed the right, then a different pattern formed in different areas. The astonishing result was that simply by looking at the patterns in the brain, the researchers could tell which button the professor would press a full six seconds before the professor felt that he had consciously decided which button to press!

The professor himself was visibly shaken by the implications of these results. Pause for a moment and think about how you would feel knowing that the conscious 'you' is not making the decisions in your life. How you would feel knowing that if I could see through your skull, I would be able to know six seconds before you did, exactly what you were going to do? Imagine what a dangerous and disconcerting place the world would be if this were possible.

But if it is not the conscious you that is making the decisions and choices, then who or what is it?

The question becomes: is the real 'You', actually your Higher Self or Daemon?

This point is vitally important as we move forward throughout the book because I want you to understand and accept that you *are* so much more than you think you are, than you may be currently expressing and capable of so much more than you may believe that you are capable of.

Electromagnetic Fields

We as human beings live in a myriad of electromagnetic fields. They can be found around the Earth, in the home and around every individual and 'thing'. You will already know about or have experience of these fields even though you may not be consciously aware of it. For example, have you ever met someone you instantly loved or hated? Have you ever walked into a room and felt the 'vibe' of anger or intuitively known that someone has had an argument in there? Have you ever felt drained of energy just by being in someone's presence?

I believe that when this happens, you are actually sensing and reading the body's electromagnetic field or Aura.

We already know that communication is only 7% language and the rest is non- verbal. I believe that a proportion of this non-verbal communication is the reading of the field.

How does this link to the Higher Self?

I believe that the Higher Self influences our decisions based on information received from the powerful heart field. The Institute of Heart Math has now shown that the electromagnetic field generated by the heart is the strongest rhythmic field produced by the body, and that it is many times more powerful than the brain. Thus if the heart's power is so immense, it would make logical sense for it to be connected to the most powerful hemisphere of the mind. The right side of the brain operates the left side of the body and the heart is obviously on the left!

For many years, researchers believed that perception and the resulting emotions were completely under the control of the brain and were a direct result of our environment. However, research now appears to show that it is, in fact, a combination of external and internal feedback from the heart firstly, which then, via the brain, communicates instructions to the body's other intelligent systems.

It is also important to note that the numbers of neural pathways going from the emotional regions in the brain to the regions responsible for cognition are far greater than the number of pathways going the opposite way.

As Doc Childre, Founder of the IHM states:

"Emotional processes can work faster than the mind; it takes a power stronger than the mind to override emotional circuitry.... It takes the power of the heart."

This is important because, if we want to alter our thought processes, beliefs and emotions, we must first determine the order in which things occur so that we can effectively alter the habitual responses. With this knowledge and a practiced degree of self-awareness we can access the critical 'choice' point at which we may choose a different and more objective response. We will look at this 'choice' point in the chapter 'Brain vs. Mind'.

What's more, researchers at the IHM have now concluded the heart has all the skills that were generally once thought to be only possessed by the brain. The heart can, through a network of connections throughout the body, act independently, learn, remember and produce feeling. And so a picture emerges of a dynamic, communicative, interrelated system that manages our emotional, perceptual reality.

The Higher Self in liaison with the heart is ultimately then, the 'I' that knows and 'sees' the bigger picture of my life, not only for myself in this body, but also for the evolution of the eternal soul energy. If this is so, not only can I trust the heart's help, but it becomes obvious that I should definitely follow its guidance.

The Ego in the Left Brain

So if the right brain is where the Higher Self resides, what then is the left brain? I believe that left brain activity is akin to the ego. Psychologists will often refer to the ego as the part of the human personality often experienced as the "Self" or "I". You will remember earlier I said that the Greeks referred to this as the Eidolon or Lower Self. For me too, the ego is the part that deals with the external world through information that has been recorded by the senses. The ego remembers, evaluates, plans, and is responsive to the physical world or environment.

The left brain is concerned with logic, planning and analysis whereas the right brain is more concerned with our artistic, creative and spiritual side. You may have experienced the ensuing head-heart battles from this relationship!

Often, it seems the ego has become a self-appointed protector in our lives, allowing us to hide from or avoid difficult and negative experiences, or parts of ourselves that we do not wish to own.

In its development, the ego has pushed to become the sole independent master of our lives. When we are too left-brained and the right brain or Higher Self is ignored, we can become too structured, limited and feel out of balance. We often reflect this in our lives by living an extremely controlled, safe, and sometimes very materialistic existence that lacks spontaneity or creativity. The left brain wants you to take the rational, logical path whereas the right brain wants to take some risks and live in the moment more.

There is another interesting case study quoted in Schiffer's book "Of Two Minds" of a man who has had the commissurotomy operation to cut the Corpus Callosum (the communication bridge between the two hemispheres).

Afterwards he states that he wants to be a draughtsperson when the left brain is questioned through the right ear. But when the right brain is questioned through the left ear, the left hand spells out with scrabble letters (as the right brain does not have access to verbal language) that it wants to be a racing driver!

Language, of which only the left side has expression in the physical world, has become so powerful in defining our world and our lives that for some of us it is not only the loudest voice but the only voice that we can hear!

Our lives are also increasingly filled with music, TV, tasks, work, chatter and anxiety that to quieten the mind and hear the Higher Self has become nigh on impossible. This is why, in my experience, so many people struggle initially with meditation.

The thoughts (or the ego) do not want to quieten down or to let go of their control!

The ego would generally like to limit our decision making and stay completely in control of everything. It is heavily invested in keeping us living a small, safe and mundane life. The creative and imaginative Higher Self, on the other hand, wishes us to fly, to experiment and to become the masters of our lives!

To my great surprise, I have joyously discovered that my Higher Self is always on hand to offer guidance. I hear Amione all the time now and welcome her wisdom. I now confidently use whatever I 'receive' in my work and teaching because it is always so wise. Sometimes I may interpret that guidance as intuition or 'inner knowing'. It thus seems obvious that I should listen to and allow myself to be guided by the one that has access to the whole picture rather than just a tiny limited part of it!

My advice then is simple — always follow your heart!

Personally, I find it incredibly comforting to know that we are far more supported by creation than we may have previously realised!

What this makes me realise is that I am ultimately an eternal soul energy and thus far more than this 'little me' in a fragile and temporary body. I am constantly receiving help and guidance throughout my life. In fact my life and all the events in it can be miraculous if I choose to label them that way. How I choose to label and judge things ultimately creates my reality and consequently how I will feel about myself and my life.

So let us now consider how this knowledge affects us and manifests itself in our everyday physical reality.

Chapter 3: Perceptual Reality

"Our deepest fear is not that we are inadequate. Our deepest fear is that we are powerful beyond measure." Marianne Williamson

Here are the four most fundamental things to remember:

1. Everything in the universe, including you, is made up of energy and energy can never be destroyed but it can change form.
2. There is always a choice and you have free will at all times.
3. Change is a fundamental, necessary and positive aspect of existence.
4. You always have access to guidance from the Higher Self.

Building on these foundations now let us now move onto the importance of your consciousness in the shaping and perception of your reality.

Many of history's most celebrated philosophers have contemplated reality and have come to the conclusion that our individual experiences may be the only reality. The American philosopher John Locke, for example, surmised that "no man's knowledge can go beyond his experience".

Locke recognised that no universal truths can be found in any baby at birth and that there are no universal truths that exist in all cultures and all people at the same time. Consequently Locke concluded that all knowledge is gained from experience.

George Berkeley, another American philosopher, proposed that our knowledge comes from our perception of ideas. However, ideas are not 'things' as such because a 'thing' must exist outside our experience. Berkeley therefore concluded that the world consists only of ideas and the minds that perceive those ideas.

We could change the language here to state that the world consists simply of consciousness and it is consciousness which perceives those ideas.

It follows then, that our experience of life is simply a construction of thought processes, experiences and perceptions.

Let us now move onto the importance of consciousness in the shaping and perception of our reality, and how we can use it to investigate who we really are.

If you were the only thing that existed, if there was not even empty space from which to differentiate yourself, how could you know anything at all about yourself? Although all of the knowledge about 'you' would exist within you, how could you experience that in any meaningful way?

The answer is that you cannot. Consciousness needs something to be conscious of.

René Descartes famously coined the phrase "I think therefore I am" but that tells us nothing other than the fact that he does exist – well, in his mind, at least!

The Oxford Dictionary defines consciousness as "the state of being aware and responsive to one's surroundings". This definition requires that there must be some surroundings to exist, of which one can be aware, in order for consciousness to arise. This tells us that consciousness needs something other than what 'it' is, from which, to differentiate itself. So here we have the first recognition of the importance of dualism in our world. Dualism is simply defined as the aspect of being dual – of being two. Therefore with the arising of anything that is, whatever else 'it' is not must exist too, if only as a potential. For example, to know that a person is short, others must exist who are taller with whom that person can be compared.

Consciousness also requires two elements for 'something' to come into existence: an object to be observed and something or someone to observe and therefore experience the said object. The recognition of the observed 'thing' causes a reflection of consciousness which is then itself observed and this cycle continues onwards. Consciousness itself, then, is a self-perpetuating feedback loop into infinity!

For example:

If I hum a note then 'some-thing' else has to have a conscious recognition of it (to hear it) that is separate from the humming. It is only at the point at which it is heard (sensed) that the hum comes into existence within physical reality (as a sound).This is the observer/observed relationship.

Therefore, there must be two parts of me — the performer of the action, which I shall call the ego, and the observer that reflects on the action, which I shall call my Higher Self.

Furthermore and using the humming example again, one could say that it is the space around the hum, the silence before and after the sound, that brings it into being as an event called the hum. Even a single word needs the space around it from which to differentiate itself.

Look at this sentence without the spaces, for example:

Ilovemylurchermorethanwordscansayorhugscanexpress.

It could even be argued that the space around the word is an *equally* important element *of* the word because without it there are just symbols which are then rendered meaningless.

The point is that we can only recognize the words when they can be differentiated from the background space which provides contrast (I.E. what the word is not):

I love my Lurcher etc.

Expanding this concept then we must have separations such as bodies in order to have a conscious experience of ourselves. Put more simply, you recognize yourself only in relationship to everything and everyone else that you are not.

However, although we immediately think in terms of polarities or opposites, duality can also be used in regard to a complementary state of existence. An obvious comparison could be made here with the Yin and Yang symbol that denotes balance with two seemingly opposite elements coming together, thus making them whole and one.

Heraclitus, an early Greek philosopher, observed that "the road up and the road down are one and the same". He noted that it is the balance of two things such as night and day that actually creates unity. After all, who can really say when day becomes night, aside from artificial demarcations of time? Night and day are actually the same one thing in motion and thus at all times are one thing but in different states of being. They are at opposite 'ends' of a 24-hour cycle but it is essentially one thing, one cycle.

Everything Is Perception

Now we understand why we must have a physical body and environment, let us look at how we use that physical environment.

If I were the only person who existed in this physical environment, I could only 'see' and thus know for sure that I was a fully physical body if, for example, I looked into a reflective medium such as water or a mirror. I could never see the back of my head without two reflective mediums for example.

We often take for granted that a mirror is simply a neutral, honest reflection of the picture that is presented before it. However, as we know from trips to the fairground, mirrors can be made to warp the view that we have of ourselves. Imagine if the only reflective material that existed was warped mirrors. We could easily become convinced that this image was truly what we looked like!

So can we ever know for sure that all the reflective mediums that exist are truly reflective? How can you ever prove that you *really* look anything like that which you are actually seeing? We know, for example, that a person suffering from anorexia nervosa may see a person who is grossly overweight in the mirror when in reality they are skeletal. As we shall see, who you are, is merely whatever your senses have decoded you to be!

It is often said that there is no way of proving that your world looks anything like mine. What I see as the colour red, for example, you may see as that which I would recognize as blue. To make it even clearer for you, colour doesn't even exist as colour as we know it!

Colour is simply the interpretation or decoding by the brain of certain vibrations and frequencies that your eyes have recorded. The brain then interprets and assigns meaning to the incoming data. Physicists say that the only thing that exists is light and thus light is actually the only thing that is real. This is obviously a profound conclusion when we relate this to the fact that most religious and spiritual theologies agree on the light being the fundamental element of 'God', angels, spirits and so on.

There is a huge electromagnetic spectrum of light that humans cannot see. In fact, we see only a tiny sliver (450-750 nanometres) in the middle of the range of what is available to see 'out there'. We are blind to the rest. The same can be said of all of our senses. Think about animals: dogs can hear sound frequencies that we cannot; others have acute levels of smell far beyond human capability.

This means that there must be much more happening in 'reality' than we are able to consciously sense and of which we as humans remain ignorant.

We know that the brain takes in information in many different formats on a daily basis. It is thought that we are subject to two million bits of information per second. However, humans are only capable of absorbing 134 bits of information per second. Our brain filters out everything that is not relevant or useful for the present moment and files the rest in the subconscious mind. Information and energy is never lost or discarded in the universe.

When you actually observe something in reality, let us say a bird flying, your eyes are not actually recording a completed scene of a bird moving through the sky. The different 'seeing' areas in your brain have to map the scene generally and then it begins to layer details — like movement, colour, depth or shape.

Scientists who have been studying patients who have damage to areas related to vision etc, have concluded that the brain builds up the shape of an object first. The brain then considers information about the features on the surface of an object. It then begins to layer in data about colour, shading, edges, and faces by their surface features. It is almost akin to building up an identikit photo. The brain is thought to match known patterns to your expectations and, I want to add, beliefs too!

Thus our reality is a reconstruction by the brain from both our consciously and subconsciously stored past data which is constantly being compared to the present moment. Our sensory systems allow only incredibly limited possibilities to exist. The fact that we are mostly matching patterns to make them fit with our old experiences severely limits the possibility of anything new arising.

So, how can you ever know for sure that you have 'interpreted' correctly that which you are actually seeing? If you ask a policeman, he will tell you that no two versions of an incident witnessed will ever be exactly the same.

This is because we filter what we see through the lenses of our perceptions, beliefs, expectations, stereotypes and maybe prejudices. Witnesses themselves will also be affected by the stress of what they saw and then the stress of trying to remember accurately any important details.

Again, we must question if there really is any objective 'reality' out there to see.

Spiritual traditions and religions have long described the world as illusion or a dream. Quantum physicists now agree that everything is energy and there is very little, if any, solid 'matter' out there at all. Atoms, the fundamental building blocks of all life, are 99.9999% vacuum which obviously is not solid! The world as we know it may indeed be a holographic or virtual projection. There is a lot of evidence now showing that how and when physical matter takes form is actually due to an observation by consciousness.

The taking of drugs such as LSD can produce hallucinations that have no physical reality but are extremely real and vivid for the person experiencing them. It is also possible to not see things that are actually there — negative hallucinations. Think about the last time that you lost your keys or glasses and your partner picked them up from in front of you!!

Consequently, nothing except your consciousness receiving and analysing data from your senses can really be proven to exist. It seems we're back to 'I think therefore I am'.

Recent developments in consciousness research have confirmed that even the sense of you as a physical body is illusory.

The wonderful BBC documentary that I mentioned earlier featured other amazing work that researched how the sense of the self can be separated from the physical body.

The program showed Professor De Sautoy sitting in a chair wearing a visor that was linked to two cameras situated behind him.

The film playing inside the visor from the cameras became his eyes, if you like. So the visor of De Sautoy was displaying the images of his physical body *appearing* to be seated in front of where he now *perceived* himself to be. So, because we are so used to believing exactly what our senses tell us, he felt as if he was actually sitting behind himself, despite being able to consciously and clearly see his own body in front of him. Later, to emphasise the depth of separation of self, the researcher swung a hammer in front of the cameras behind where De Sautoy was actually sitting and Dr Sautoy was fooled into reacting as if the hammer was going to smash into his chest. This proves that De Sautoy truly believed that he was where the cameras were placed. Thus for all intents and purposes, his consciousness or sense of "I" was now fully within the cameras. I found this profoundly disturbing because if our senses can be tricked so easily, it means you could actually be a brain in a glass jar having your senses stimulated artificially.

How could you tell the difference? In some ways, this is what the popular Matrix films depicted (in more dramatized form).

The Matrix is a computer-generated reality program run by an alien race which is plundering the earth. Each human is 'asleep' in a watery cocoon. They are also wired up to an artificial reality computer system and have their senses stimulated whilst a computer-generated film of reality is played to them. They are oblivious to the truth and believe fully that they are living a 'real' life with real experiences.

Some years ago, I had the experience of 'Alien 4D' at one of the large American theme parks in Florida. I sat in a very narrow chair that vibrated to simulate movement and had on a visor that showed me an extremely horrific and disturbing film of aliens on a space craft chasing me around.

The experience was so real to me, that to this day, I can still remember and vividly 'see' the drooling alien eyeball to eyeball with me. I remember feeling its breath on my face, which was being created by steam or spray from a gadget in the chair I think. I was truly terrified. The soundtrack was being played so close to my ears, which made it feel as if it really was my reality in that moment. Now of course, on some level I was obviously still in touch with the part of me that knew I had just voluntarily walked into the theatre. Therefore, I didn't have the heart attack that I am sure that I would have had, *if*, I had experienced this scenario in my regular everyday reality. Nevertheless, I did experience a range of very vivid, fear-related physical sensations!

Think about this, however. Had you been born straight into that theatre and situation with no knowledge of the world outside that environment, how could you have known that that experience was not your 'real' life?

You may have seen the film 'The Truman Show', which is on a similar theme, where a man has been born into a closed film set. Because Truman has never experienced or known that there is anything other than this as his home environment, he believes that the world of the theatrical set is reality! Something or someone has to come into that environment from the outer world in order for Truman to be able to wake up to the lie.

Is it not scary that it can be demonstrated so easily that you are wherever your senses tell you that you are? Even more unsettling, you are whatever or whoever your sensory feedback mechanisms interpret the data to be. Who is really sitting at the editor's table putting reality together into a coherent picture for us? Who is it that is deciding what that range of incoming data best fits?

I am not saying that 'nothing' exists, but I am proposing that our local reality at the level of the collective and individual consciousness may be thought-based only.

Now for some people this is so counter- intuitive that they will dismiss it out of hand — that is fine. For some people, this will be interesting but not make a huge impact on their day-to-day behaviour — this is also fine. For others, like me, they will want to exploit the possibilities to the max.

Wherever you are on that scale is absolutely fine because all I am trying to do is to loosen your grip on the idea of life being set in stone; that life is something that happens to you and that you are powerless to influence. Whatever is the true nature of existence, even mainstream science is confirming that it is profoundly affected by consciousness, attention, vibration and our thoughts. This is, in fact, all we need to know in order to understand the concepts that I am presenting here.

I want to encourage you to start to accept that you really can take control of yourself, your world and your relationships by taking control of your thoughts, beliefs and behaviours. This also means, however, that you can no longer claim to be a victim of the fickle hand of fate!

Finally, please allow me to relate the story of my 'Strawberry Moment' to illustrate the incredible importance of choice and truth in one's life.

I am a dedicated and unashamed worshipper of the sun. Whenever the sun is out, I am out and usually in my lovely garden. In this particular summer, I had sat in the same spot every day that week and on the day in question I had been sitting out for about twenty minutes.

My life was just beginning to emerge from the dark night of depression and I was seeing so many coincidences and synchronistic events that on some days I felt like life was truly miraculous. I absolutely loved that feeling. As I sat there sipping my tea, I suddenly noticed a fully-grown, bright red strawberry hanging over the edge of a flower pot by my legs and to me it seemed like it had literally just appeared out of nowhere!

I was confused because I had never planted strawberries. I had never seen any sign in the preceding days of this fruit growing. And yet here it was – a juicy, luscious, fully-grown strawberry. My favourite fruit too. It was as if it had just appeared as my personal gift from God, my miracle. I became very excited and started texting my friends and family.

Now I am sure that most of them read my text and just rolled their eyes.

No-one seemed to understand my sudden excitement about the world or share my new-found delight in everything around me. My son actually still to this day thinks that I am having a mid-life crisis!

Anyway, I digress. My oldest but most cynical friend rang me and informed me quite assuredly that a bird must have flown over and poohed the seeds into my pot.

I fell from walking on air to crash and burn in the space of a few minutes. "Damn", I thought, "there is a rational explanation after all."

However, as I sat there, I began to wonder why I had not seen any evidence of the strawberry growing and developing before that moment. Then it hit me and I suddenly realised that no-one held the bag of truth. My friend could not prove her case because of the afore-mentioned anomalies and I could not prove that it was a miracle. This seemingly insignificant incident became a major turning point in my life because I suddenly realised that I could choose whichever version of the story served me best.

I could choose to live in the mastery and magic of life or in the mundaneness of existence.

I realised in that moment that simply because there may have been a rational explanation for an event, it did not necessarily make it true. Sometimes we 'know' something instinctively, but we have forgotten how to trust ourselves.

By ignoring our own tremendous sense of intuition, we often end up living the beliefs, fears and values of everyone around us!

The difference between how the two worlds felt was enough to ensure that in that very moment, I made a life-changing shift of focus. I decided that I would always 'believe' the explanation or point of view that was most beneficial for my health and well-being regardless! I now choose to live in the mastery. The truth, I now realise, is only ever a matter of my perception - as is everything else in life.

The Buddha Siddhartha Gautama advised us all "Believe nothing no matter where you read it, who said it, unless it agrees with your own reason".

Chapter 4: The Reality Mirror –

Life inside the Mirror Ball!
"Peace comes from within. Do not seek it without." Buddha

There is a lovely Japanese parable that is called 'The House of a Thousand Mirrors' and it goes something like this. A dog inadvertently strays into the house of mirrors. He becomes very frightened by all the 'other' dogs that appear to be staring back at him and begins to bark aggressively. Obviously, the 'other' 1,000 dogs then start barking back at him and he becomes so frightened that he runs away and hides forever. Some years later, another dog strays into the house, but is so happy to see all these 'other' friends that he jumps for joy and is then delighted to see 1,000 happy friends playing along with him.

This is such a wonderfully simple but poignant analogy for how our lives are actually working. Many of you will clearly see the analogy of 'what you give out, you get back' which is abundantly obvious here and we shall cover more in the chapter on the Law of Attraction. But this story is really about the multitude of mirrors. The first element in my TOUR empowerment system is to look into the reality mirror at what is really happening to you in that moment.

It helps me to imagine that I live inside a huge mirror ball. In fact, I ended up buying a giant mirror ball that now sits in front of my living room window. I did not know why I bought it at the time, but I now realise that I was trying to show myself something very profound. A mirror ball is a ball that is hung from the ceiling in discos and clubs and is made, as the name suggests, from tiny tiled mirrors.

When lights are projected onto mirror balls, they reflect many smaller lights in various locations, shapes and sizes out across a room. When the sunlight hits my ball, the room is brought to life with magic little discs of light.

Now because these tiny mirrored tiles are all at slightly different angles and in slightly different positions, if I look into the ball or move around it my reflection appears differently in each of the tiles.

Were I to imagine that I lived inside the mirror ball, I could project aspects of myself outwards and see them reflected back to me slightly differently from each tile. This is akin to the mechanism psychologists call projection which essentially allows us to see what is going on in our subconscious minds by externalizing it.

We are said to be constantly projecting our deepest emotions, rejected character traits, thoughts and beliefs onto others or our environment. This process allows us to see and experience a relationship with all aspects of our true selves both objectively and subjectively.

This mechanism then gives us an opportunity to accept, heal or reject aspects of our personalities.

The famous Swiss psychoanalyst Carl Jung described the place occupied by all the traumas and upsets that have occurred in our lives as The Shadow. He describes The Shadow as "An unconscious aspect of the personality which the conscious ego does not recognize in itself".

Often we tend to reject or want to remain ignorant of the least desirable aspects of our personality and thus we hide them within The Shadow.

The mechanism of projection works in many different ways. By projecting and then seeing my rejected traits in a range of other people, I can react to and judge the trait objectively without emotional attachment. I am then able to make a decision about whether or not I would like to have that trait. Alternatively, I can project out and have a subjective, relational experience of my traits and how they affect me emotionally.

I had an intense lesson about this many years ago when I was working in an office and at the same time trying to work my way through the final stages of depression. I saw one person at work as being the sole source of all my problems. I blamed this person and his attitude towards me, for *my* unhappiness in the job. There were many things I didn't like about him, but for the purposes of this example I will focus one issue, and that was his laziness as I perceived it. I resented this man and this feeling was enhanced by the fact that I was the 'junior' in the office but older than him. I had a belief that one should always respect ones elders but felt totally disrespected by him.

Anyway, I read somewhere that everyone presents you with an opportunity to see things that you do not want to own about yourself, and that you should list everything that annoys you about that person in order to explore this. So I listed 10 things about this man and decided to work on them one at a time. When he was lazy in my opinion, I learned to say to myself, "Well, I'm lazy too sometimes so how can I blame him for something that I do?" and let it go. Jesus' teaching that, only the person who is without sin should cast any stone, ran constantly through my mind!

As I worked through the list, an amazing thing happened. Not only did I find my attitude about this man changing but I also changed my attitude about the job too. I came to see that I was the problem. I was going into the office angry about my life and causing an awful atmosphere and others, consciously or not, were reacting to this. When I started to feel better about myself and about my life, the job and everything else around me changed too.

So in fact the only 'lazy' person I had to work on was me! I had been trying to change the scowling face in the mirror not realising that I needed to stop scowling!

"Have you ever noticed that whenever there is a problem…*you* are there?"

I love this quote (from the book Zero Limits by Joe Vitale) because it really is the crux to taking full responsibility for all of your creations. If you are the problem then you are also the solution. This question really brings it home to me on all levels that *I am* creating all of my problems.

To start taking full responsibility for your life you have to accept the following truths:

A. You are the problem BUT also the solution.

B. A problem should be relabelled as a challenge or an opportunity.

C. The person who is causing you problems is either the reflection of your traits in the mirror or is giving you an opportunity to learn how to deal with these traits successfully.

D. The solution is to stop scowling in the mirror and the reflection that you see will stop scowling back!

E. Forgive this person, forgive yourself and thank them for playing 'that' role for you so that you could learn and grow. They are your spiritual teacher.

I was horrified to learn that I was the causing all the problems in the office and very grateful when my colleagues accepted my apologies a year or so later. To apologise was a real step towards owning and releasing the whole situation fully for me. It obviously took a lot of courage, but facing that fear and overcoming it was incredibly empowering in my life going forward.

Sometimes we are creating situations that may initially appear to be negative or challenging, but are actual treasure chests of learning. Part of my working through depression was getting to know which traits were hidden within me that I did not accept consciously, and uncovering a raft of hidden belief programs. For example, I have a belief system that links self-worth, high self-esteem and being a good person, to work. The reason I had taken this particular job was because the hours suited being a single mum, but I became demotivated by working at a low level and beneath my ability. I came to realise that it was my belief programming on this which needed addressing.

I knew I was worthy and capable of more and so did my Higher Self. The negative emotions I was experiencing were because I was out of alignment with the greatness of my eternal soul energy.

As the book progresses, you will see that this alignment with the greatness of who you really are on a spiritual level is crucial to wellbeing. I could not change the external world by trying to change this one individual. My work was to heal myself and to realise what I already knew deep down inside, which is that I was so much more than I was allowing myself to be in that situation. Bluntly, that I was better than that job and that behaviour!

My thought pattern before doing all this self-development work was that this person was lazy and that that was a fact. I later realised that whether that is true or not for him is actually nothing to do with me. I do not have the right to judge anyone else. Whoever or whatever he was, or was not, was for him to work on not me. His perceived laziness was in fact just my judgement, my label, and my opinion. I came to accept that I could only work on and change myself. Have you ever tried to change anyone else anyway? It never works.

Pause for a moment and think again about who is present in your life at the moment and what they are reflecting back to you both positively and negatively.

In the twelve-step program at Alcoholics Anonymous, they have a mantra that says "If you spot it, you got it".

If 'you got it' then you are likely to find yourself reacting adversely to that quality in someone else as subconsciously you recognise yourself and initially fight to reject it. I am sorry to tell you this, but the people that you struggle most with are really aspects of yourself in other clothing, the warped mirror image if you like!

It is essential, however, that we do not allow ourselves to reject any part of ourselves completely. We are all a mix of positive and negative aspects.

So I suggest that you have look around your life and look in particular at those people whom you dislike or judge most harshly. These are the very people that you should now thank most profusely for leading you to the pot of gold within you.

How the Mirror Works

Let us try to understand more fully this concept that everyone is a mirror and some details of how it works in our everyday life.

Firstly, ask yourself this: How do you know that you exist today? What information or experiences make you so sure of your existence?

*Notice if you say anything that includes knowing yourself in relationship to, or in comparison with, anything or anyone else.

To be able to discover and learn consciously who we are, there has to be an interplay, movement, adversaries and things that we are not. By using other people as reflective mirrors, upon which we can project aspects of ourselves, we provide ourselves with opportunities to know, heal or release these traits.

Ultimately, I believe that my life and experiences are created by a continuous interplay with each person with whom I have a relationship. I can objectively and subjectively experience having, being or receiving the consequences of any particular trait and how that actually feels. Every relationship I have thus gives me an opportunity to accept, heal or change who I believe I am and perhaps who I would prefer to be in the future.

In some ways, this is why we tend to marry people who are very similar in character to our fathers or mothers. By choosing a person who resembles one of our parents, we then have an opportunity through our new relationship to work out issues and problems that we had in the parental relationship. We have another opportunity to heal. We choose that partner because subconsciously they remind us in some way of our mother or father. For example, if a man had a mother who was very domineering, he might as an adult choose to marry a domineering woman so that he can work through his issues of disempowerment.

As an easy example, I only recently realised that one of the things I admired about my ex-husband was his work ethic. He

44

was very hard-working, but as a result he was often away from the home.

So was my dad! I wanted my husband to be at home more just as I had wanted my father to be at home more and for him to spend more time with me. As this issue had never been resolved with my dad, marrying a man who was also frequently absent gave me the opportunity to heal, accept or own the issue within a new relationship.

At its core, this issue is really about my ability to be happy unconditionally and to not expect my happiness to be provided by others. If I failed to heal this issue with my husband then I would end up recreating the same problem with another person in another way. The scene may look completely different but the underlying issue would essentially be the same. That is essentially what happened in my life until I learned that I had that program running.

So we have established that the process of projection gives us the opportunity to own and heal the aspects of ourselves and 'painful' events in our past of which we may be unaware or fail to accept exist within us.

However there are two ways that projection works and it need not necessarily be one or the other, but could be a mix of both. Firstly we can draw to us a person who needs what we have to give and vice versa.

I love the idea that one can only teach that which one has to learn themselves. For example, I am amazed how many clients I see with an issue that I may currently be working on in that period.

I know that I have drawn them to me in order to give that therapy to myself also. As you give, you receive!

Secondly we can imagine that everyone and everything is a blank screen upon which we project exactly what we require of them or it. Here is a clear example of how reality can be a blank screen and how two people can experience that same environment completely differently because of their personal filters of perception.

When an old partner and I started going out, we used to attend a social club. I would see lovely people dancing and having a great time because, as he would say, my world is joyous and full of bunnies.

He, on the other hand, working in security, basically saw trouble everywhere. The physical reality was the same for both of us, but because of the filters of our perceptions he saw troublesome and unfriendly people and I could only see wonderful people. I only saw people dancing and laughing whilst he only 'saw' the CCTV cameras!

Early Programming
Sadly, most of us are trying to escape from some of the reflections that we see because we do not want to accept that this is what we really look like. Or perhaps we genuinely do not even recognize ourselves in those images.

We may not connect the way we are now with the way we were brought up and the beliefs introduced to us when we were young. Think of it like this. If you plant a daffodil bulb, it looks nothing like the flower it becomes many months later. So if you were not the one who originally planted the bulb and of course cannot see the bulb beneath the soil, you could potentially fail to link the flower with the bulb.

Now before I go on, I must make it clear that we are not blaming our parents in any way for who we are today. I know that I certainly did not receive a manual on how to be a good parent—or even just how to do it reasonably well. The truth is though that as children, up until a certain age at least, we believe everything we are told without judgement.

As a child sees it, when our parents criticise us, they are not just reprimanding us for a particular behaviour but also saying that we are wrong, bad, not likeable and thus not loved. Consequently, if as children we were reprimanded in any way, we could potentially spend the rest of our lives attempting to prove that we are in fact lovable and likeable. Teenagers are a good example of this.

At that age, we are so desperate to be liked and to fit in that we behave in ways that later we realise were not necessarily in our best interests.

For example, an adult may strive to be super-successful professionally because his or her father criticised his or her childhood achievements. Maybe this drive stemmed from a time when the father showed he was disappointed or made a throwaway comment about the child's sporting skills for example.

As an adult, this person may strive for success upon success because subconsciously all he/she wants is to earn the father's love and approval. The belief program for this person may be 'winning or success equals 'love.'

Obviously, the parent will not have given the child negative belief programs consciously so we are not discussing blame here. What I am doing is simply highlighting the mechanism that affects children and young children particularly. If eventually the adult in the above example became a top tennis player and won Wimbledon, then on the face of it this would be a positive event. But if the father didn't acknowledge this success because he considered tennis to be valueless, then the adult child would still feel a failure, unfulfilled and unloved.

All events are in fact neutral, but as young children we lack the emotional intelligence, critical faculty and discernment to be able to separate ourselves from our emotional response to events. We cannot even separate ourselves as individuals from our parents before the age of 18 months.

Therefore, as babies we share the same experiences, beliefs and emotions of everyone around us, particularly our parents. The judgements and rejection that we experience around events become faithfully recorded without censorship. These then colour our perception and beliefs about the world, going forward in our life.

Remember that events look and feel very different from a child's eye view.

Hypnotherapists are taught that the root cause of many issues that people have is to be found in early childhood—let us say before the age of seven—because up until that age children accept everything that is said by their trusted elders as an absolute truth. We rely on our parents for our very survival and thus to not accept everything that they espouse as truth could potentially affect our ability to survive. Consequently, all of the learning, advice and experiences that we encounter in early childhood get diligently recorded as beliefs and programs in the brain without censorship.

Later, as we become aware of (and often ashamed of) our negative qualities and socially unacceptable impulses, they start to 'leak out'. If we vehemently do not want to own these qualities or impulses we may even become the most outspoken 'champion' against them because we feel the emotion around them so strongly. We want them out of sight and out of mind because although subconsciously we know the issue is ours, consciously we are not ready to own it.

Maybe a child is ridiculed for wanting attention or 'acting the clown', for instance. Or it could be that a child is humiliated for crying or punished for being angry. Eventually these children gradually learn to repress the traits or behaviours that they were criticised for and which caused them such emotional pain. They carry this repression into their adult life.

I think it is important, however, to recognize that there are likely to also be positive aspects to these perceived negative traits. For example, in the above cases, the ability to make people laugh and have fun is valuable in social situations while the ability to express emotions fully can actually be very healthy. Sometimes, even traits which we ourselves have labelled as negative can actually be very positive ones.

Take selfishness, for example. This is a trait that most people would label as negative. However, to be selfish could actually also mean to be focused, independent and self-honouring.

There is nothing wrong with the trait itself; it is only the way that it is expressed or judged that can make it appear negative.

It is essential therefore that we never reject a particular trait completely, but instead look for the positive aspect of it and at how we can use it more wisely. Just by being more mindful about how we express it, selfishness can be added to our tools for success.

The subconscious mind may attempt to allow a person to see his shadow or unconscious beliefs within dreams and/or present it as a myriad of different symbols and forms.

Interactions with The Shadow in dreams can also allow us to shed light on our real state of mind. This is why I always suggest to my students and clients to keep a journal of their dreams and explore what their dreams are trying to tell them. I ask people to interpret what the image means to them because different images mean different things to different individuals. If you get stuck, however, there are excellent dream dictionaries available from which to start your explorations.

Dream states can also be used to facilitate whatever healing work we wish to do on ourselves.

We are all in this huge relationship together because everything is entwined and one. We must accept that we as humans are naturally predisposed towards rejecting and avoiding negative emotions and feelings. Although honouring and expressing our negative emotions may feel counterintuitive, it is vital for our physical health and wellbeing to be able to do so.

Great peace can be found in the acceptance of your own power and creations. Never forget that if you are the problem, then you are also the solution. There is nowhere to hide from the fact that you are the creator of your reality.

You cannot cherry pick only the positive scenarios to own as your creation. Nor can you run away from the problems that you are creating because wherever you run, you take yourself with you. It is impossible to shake free of your physical or mental shadow!

Chapter 5: Happy to the CORE
"The sky behind the clouds is always blue" Anon

So far we have discovered that the following aspects are important elements in understanding how our personal realities are operating.

1. All events and people are neutral until we layer judgement upon them.

2. You create your reality based on your perceptions, beliefs and expectations.

3. You are the writer, director, producer, lead actor and entire cast in your 'play' of life.

4. Everyone out there is a mirror or teacher for you.

5. We use events, people and objects as tools to help us learn about ourselves, our world and our programming.

Now let me introduce the next set of principles that I believe you need to be aware of when you are consciously creating your reality in this play of life. We'll start with assertiveness.

How can you constantly follow your excitement if you have to limit your choices or responses in deference to other people?

In order to consciously create your own reality fully, you have to believe in yourself, be totally focused on your goals and to own what you are manifesting. Assertiveness is a key factor in being able to do that because you have to be able to assert firmly in every situation exactly what it is that you prefer, how you want to be, what you want to do and have, without deferring to anyone else's beliefs or judgments.

I believe the ability to say yes or no as a matter of free choice and without any sense of guilt is the key to true assertiveness. We often defer to other people's point of view, rules and wishes because we have been conditioned that it is polite and good manners to do so. We judge ourselves as 'good' people and feel loved if we constantly put other people first. We will deal with this issue again later in the book, but for now I want to make the point that when we do things from a place of 'should' rather than desire, we give away our power and just end up feeling resentful. This is the reason that when we cannot be assertive or honour our own needs, the resulting emotion feels so bad and drags us down so far.

My belief is that you are not alive to be beholden to any other adult. You are here to live your life and have your experiences. We must all take responsibility for ourselves and our choices.

In order to find true peace and happiness we must all practice conscious self-is-ness.

As we have already seen, you are one with everything and everyone and thus you are as good, equal to and just as deserving as anyone else out there. So why would your opinion or viewpoint count for less than anyone else's? No one holds the bag of truth. In a universe that is built around the notion of free will and choice, how can anything be deemed right or wrong, true or false? There surely only can be that which is right or wrong for you or right or wrong for me. And most of us have a fully functional moral compass to keep us on the right track for that.

Why should you feel that you are wrong in some way, less knowledgeable or less deserving than any other bag of cells out there? After all, that's what we really are. We are all the same underneath.

Often you may be less assertive because you have not consciously thought about or been shown your beautiful inner essence. If you have never been taught that you are a powerful creator of your reality then you may not have been given the tools with which to change. In some ways, helping you to acquire these tools is one of the main purposes of this book.

Most importantly, as you continue your personal development work you will find that there are old subconscious belief programs running that constantly reinforce your negative thoughts and feelings. That is why a little later we are going to use what I call the CORE strategies and TOUR worksheets to uncover these hidden background programs and to remove them from the computer.

However, please be aware that once you have obtained the tools for change and uncovered the subconscious beliefs, to not act upon them can no longer be called ignorance but choice!

Labels

We tend to define ourselves as a physical body that is separated from others by space and we then layer on quite arbitrary labels which redefine us in different roles, states of being and environments. For example, I may define myself in this way: I am Theresa, a human, hypnotherapist, a woman, white, short, generally happy etc.

Often, we become so absorbed in language and labels that we forget that these are merely arbitrary tools that were developed so that we could differentiate between ourselves and different objects. These labels originally developed to enable us to operate cohesively as a society or community that was becoming ever more complex.

As the late American philosopher Richard Porty concluded, we cannot have a conscious knowledge about a dog, for example, outside of our thoughts and thus labels about a dog. You could experience a 'dog' but without thought and by implication language, it would be no more than an in the moment experience through the senses. You only 'know' that that animal is called a dog by a parent perhaps labelling it as a dog for you.

As children, we have to learn about the nature of 'dogginess' as we grow and experience dogs and understand that they have four legs, a tail, that they bark etc. We need to develop in our minds a concept about 'dogginess' with language, labels and pictures in order to operate in a world with dogs.

Unfortunately, many of us have come to believe that the labels given to us through language are who we are. We make decisions and judgements every day about who we are and we also do the same to others. It is almost like walking around sticking post it notes on everything, but believing that the note defines the object. If someone sticks a post it with the word 'plonker' onto my forehead and other people constantly read the note out loud, I may start to believe that I am a 'plonker' thinking 'Everyone is saying it so it must be true'.

The brain programs beliefs by repetition. We will look into this in depth a little later. What I have to remember, however, is that I always have a choice.

I can remove the note, ignore it and or allow it to define me.

It is good to remember that a label is just a neutral string of symbols, letters, words or tools created simply for the purpose of differentiation.

If I call you 'grimgashca', I am sure that you would not really be bothered. But if I called you stupid you would have a certain emotional reaction to that label. Words are essentially neutral. They are essentially meaningless until we layer meaning upon them with our judgements and beliefs and then accept them as absolute truths. You may remember the old adage from school that 'sticks and stones may break my bones but names can never hurt me'.

It may be worth revisiting this as an adult because it certainly can be a powerful lesson in separating oneself from the negative labels that we and others pin upon us.

I remember vividly asking one of my students to stop labelling himself as depressed because that language is the way that you program your brain and this then becomes your reality! This student was allowing the label of depression to excuse certain behaviours and feelings. He saw himself as someone who was depressed—the label had come to define him and his acceptance of the label affected his vibration and limited his ability to become anything else. It is not only language and labels though with which we become defined by others. The 'vibe' that we give off and which others react too is incredibly important. This vibration also affects and colours how you will behave and feel in relation to others.

How you hold and present yourself in life physically does affect how people treat you. I remember watching an episode of Oprah Winfrey where she interviewed a security expert about how women could keep themselves safe at night on the streets. If you were an attacker, the expert asked, would you pick on the person who was hunched over and looked scared and fragile, or the person striding along with their head held high?

His point was that sometimes in life we are unconsciously screaming out that we are victims. When this happens, we attract situations that reinforce or allow us to play out our victim-hood. And the sad thing is that that vibration is so far away from the greatness that your soul knows you as. The negative feeling of victim-hood is almost like a call from the soul to remember who you really are and to own your greatness.

It is said that we make our decision about another person within the first 30 seconds of meeting them. Speed dating was created around this concept and the fact that you have just seconds to make a good impression. What are we basing our initial judgements on if it is not partially at least the vibrational field and body language of the other person?

I always tell people going to interviews to give a firm handshake and to make eye contact with the person interviewing them. It is my belief that you make a spiritual connection in that way with every person you meet as the eyes are indeed the windows of the soul. And because we are all connected, the other person will immediately feel like they 'know and trust' you without consciously knowing why.

I believe that we are all beautiful spiritual essences and perfect creations, not perfect people but perfect creations of the universe. The real you is so much more than your physical body or the artificial personality that you have constructed around it. Just think for a moment about how different you may act; at work as opposed to at home, with friends socially as opposed to formal situations, with your children as opposed to when you are with your parents.

Which one of these multitude of personalities is the real you? The universe has imbued us all with the wonderful gift of free will and so in reality you could choose to be any one of these personalities or indeed none of them. You play many roles in your 'play' of life. You can choose to reinvent the character that you are today if you so wish and many people actually do so.

I know for example that I am a completely different person now to the person I was ten, five or even one year ago. Even after this reading session, you become a different person because you will have learned new things and the wiring of your brain is changing. Remember that the entire physical body is completely regenerated over a two-year period. So, again, who are you really?

But with the right to choose who you want to be comes the responsibility to be totally accepting of who we already are and the fact that we will never be perfect. Nor should we ever want to be perfect because that leaves no room to grow and develop. Stagnation and death would be sure to follow!

Accepting that you are not perfect in itself allows for the love and acceptance of self to flourish. And to love yourself unconditionally means exactly that—that you love yourself whatever the conditions, that you love yourself no matter what you have done or how things have turned out.

I think that loving the self unconditionally means being able to take full responsibility for what you have said or done, but also being able to say: I did the best that I could with the knowledge and ability that I had at that time.

I want you to make this your mantra should guilt or regret ever arise in your life. The past is the past anyway and thus guilt or regret serve no purpose and are unable to change anything now.

"I know that I did the best that I could with the knowledge and ability that I had at that time."

And who can ask or expect anything more than that? This is how I reconcile the disappointment I sometimes feel in myself as a parent although I should add that my son says he does not know what I am talking about if I ever mention my doubts to him. If you feel that you have done something wrong or you are unhappy with your behaviour, take the courageous route and ask the other person their view on it. You may be suffering for no reason. We are always our own harshest critic!!

If it turns out there is a problem, do whatever you can to fix it and then let it go. Ask yourself: Was my intention good? If the answer is yes, give yourself a break! You cannot be responsible for how things turn out 'out there'. Everybody is reacting from their own point of reference and seeing life through the filters of their beliefs and programs. You will never know how, why or what anyone else is taking from you. Think about my work colleague who could have had no idea that my anger towards his laziness was actually an issue of my self-esteem and lack of motivation.

When you are sure that your intentions are always good, you have a strong sense of self-belief and self-acceptance then, by consequence, confidence can develop naturally.

Confidence and assertiveness are qualities that allow you to stand strongly in your own shoes and say I am a good person, I matter and, most importantly, I do not care what you think. Confidence says clearly to another person that yes, you are entitled to your opinion but I am able to choose whether to listen to it or not.

As I have already said, I am all for promoting self-is-ness. This is not the same thing as selfishness. It is not something that you do that causes another person deliberate pain because you would do that from a negative stance. Self-is-ness is about honouring the value of you!

The CORE Strategy
Let us now look a little more closely at the four simple CORE keys to happiness.

These are the four CORE keys that I have found to living happily.

C is for Confidence

Some people think that confidence is a magical like quality that you are born with. "You either got it or you don't kid!" My definition is simple:

Confidence occurs when you really do not care what anyone else thinks about you.

Just imagine for a moment how differently you would act, what you could do, who you would be and what you could achieve if you just gave up thinking that there was anyone else out there whose judgement of you mattered? Or that there was anyone else out who had a right to judge you anyway! We are all one, all the same, simply bags of cells.

There is a saying 'fake it til you make it' and this is what many successful people do. Confidence is a mind-set. It is a state of being that says I am ok as I am. Confidence is not giving a fig about what anyone else has to say about you!

O is for Opinion

Other people's judgements and criticisms are just their opinion - no more and no less. You cannot please all of the people all of the time.

There is not, and I am sure will never be, a person in existence that absolutely everyone loves because we all like and want different things and so it should be. The acceptance of that point alone will end your suffering right now! We do not all want strawberry jam, some of us want raspberry!

Everyone 'out there' is an aspect of you anyway and you will see that they are there simply to give you an opportunity to reflect upon *you*. Often, we only reflect on our behaviour or relationship to one another if someone else passes comment. Change judgments to opinions and be bothered (or not) only once you have reflected and decided how you feel. Make an informed choice about whether to accept another's opinion *or not.* Question and reflect objectively on everything.

No-one has the right to tell you how to act or to be. No-one else is ever automatically right. And no-one can affect you unless you allow them to! Say or think to yourself, "That's ok. That's just your opinion - Whatever!' And, by the way, you are not here to make anyone else happy. It is their responsibility to do that for themselves!

R is for Right? Who cares? Who knows?

"Is it better to be right or happy?"
We waste so much of our energy and time trying to prove that we are right. Who cares? Caring is a sign of the ego at work. It really is not important most of the time. So fight battles only when it really is an important life-changing or life enhancing moment. Once I started practising the mantra above, I became really happy, really quickly, believe me. I now know that keeping my vibration high is far more important than feeling superior. At the end of the day, I may be wrong and often there is no truth out there anyway. It is also good to remember that sometimes both viewpoints can be right. It can be this or that OR this *and* that! Sometimes, the answer is just yes to both!

E is for Excitement

The quickest way to get happy and to stay there is to just keep moving towards the next best thing, every single minute of every single day. We often slavishly follow our 'shoulds' when what we really want to do is something a lot more exciting. Be free. Make choices. Be daring. Take more risks. Live on the edge a little more. Remember that 'you matter!' Your happiness is all that really counts. Begin to change your language from anxiety, stress and fear to excitement, enthusiasm or even anticipation. If you stop to feel emotions and physical sensations without labelling them, you will begin to realise that they are just neutral, physical sensations. It is the label that you lay over the feeling that makes it positive or negative. The physical reaction is caused by you judging the event in a certain way.

The Power of the Emotions

Now I realise that if you are new to this work, to ask you to take your power back, to take full responsibility for your choices and to open yourself to the full force of your emotions is a big ask. However, it is the understanding and acceptance of self that will allow you to take control over your emotions and to use them positively and healthily.

Some people may feel uncomfortable if they have spent a lifetime being told that big boys don't cry or to pull themselves together if they show any emotion, but these are actually programs of powerlessness. Some people, who consider themselves to be very spiritual or have done a lot of self-development work, can sometimes fear allowing the expression of any negative emotion.

Tears, lashing out and shouting are all natural release valves for pressure in the system. If you don't honour them then not only are you rejecting an obvious part of yourself but you will be arguing with what is. If you are angry then by knowing that you are angry, it is already too late to stop it. You are angry — but now you are at a choice point about how and when to express that anger. This is where your place of power lies.

So what do I mean by choice point?

For me, there is a difference between responding as a controlled, positive action with considered choice- *and reacting*. Responding could mean taking considered action or choosing not to respond at all. Reacting on the other hand means negative or uncontrolled behaviour. In any moment you have a choice whether to allow another person to affect you. Anger management teachers, for example, may tell people to 'break the state' by taking a breath and counting to 10 before responding. That would be the choice point.

The recognition that you actually have the choice is totally freeing.

Free will! Your choice! Choice is power.

We will look more at the choice point later in the chapter Brain vs. the Mind.

At the end of the day, all emotion is simply sensation with judgement or labels layered over it. The next time you are experiencing powerful emotion, try just sitting with it and watch what happens when you dispense with the label or the story.

It is a difficult thing to do at first, but with practice you will see that all emotions are just sensations designed to grab your attention. All emotions are simply reflective of our place of power in any given moment. They are simply information or guidance and nothing to be frightened of.

Negative emotions are also a fail-safe mechanism to release pressure in the system. This is particularly the case with tears. Tears are made of water which cleanses, heals and refreshes.

They literally wash away the pain and cleanse the soul. Just as we rid the body of excess energy by jumping for joy, we need to release emotions like anger physically and mentally. If we think about emotions as mere energy, we can see that when someone argues with us and makes us angry it is because they steal our power and our energy. After losing an argument, we usually feel drained and low. That is why we want to lash out because we need to regain our energy and momentum.

We fail to deal with and express all of our emotions at our peril.

However, it is always vital to acknowledge that these thoughts, emotions or beliefs are not you. Never forget that ultimately you are the soul energy and that these beliefs and emotions are merely the 'clothes' that you are wearing at this moment in your physical experience. If you do not like what you see then you can easily change.

As I came to realise when I was depressed, depression is one of the lowest vibrations because at the time you feel completely powerless to change the situation.

This sense of victim- hood then becomes a self-fulfilling prophecy. I learned through that experience that true power always rests in taking ownership for all of ones actions. The acceptance of this is the basic key to happiness.

Allowing yourself to be a little vulnerable, to be less than perfect, to accept that you are doing the best you can in every moment (and thus it must be good enough because it is your best) actually opens the doorway to love and self-respect.

However there is a difference between being vulnerable from the place of lack of self-love, weakness or victim- hood as opposed to being vulnerable from a place of personal power. The first makes another person responsible for one's happiness whilst the latter comes from knowing and accepting full responsibility for one's own happiness.

Allowing the self to be vulnerable also allows other people the opportunity to show that they do love and care about us.

It also allows them to give us the help and guidance that we can only get from others who have the objective view on our situations. Vulnerability also allows us the space to ask for help from the Higher Self that only wants the best for us. When we open our hearts to vulnerability, the universe opens its heart to us.

Let us end this chapter by revisiting Marianne Williamson's quote: "Our deepest fear is not that we are inadequate. Our deepest fear is that we are powerful beyond measure"

It is time for us all to take our power back, to own the wonderful creations that we are as the microcosm of the universe. We are not only these physical bodies. We are not the labels and characters that we play. We deserve to be loved because we are lovable. We can allow ourselves to be less than perfect because we are designed that way. We all are less than perfect because we need room to grow. We can allow ourselves to be vulnerable so that others can help themselves by helping us. We can allow others to heal through our acceptance of their ignorance and by owning our reflection from them. We can allow others to be right and we can allow ourselves to be happy.

Finally, we can use all of these things to stand strong and to assert:

I think, therefore, I matter!

Chapter 6: Law of Attraction (LOA)

"Act as if what you do makes a difference. It does!" William James

The 19th century philosopher William James came to the above conclusion through the following thought experiment:

If you are lost and alone in the forest, you have two choices. You can believe:

1. That there is no way out and that you will starve and die. The consequential action is that you sit down, give up hope and die.

2. That there is a way out that leads to food and shelter. The consequential action is that you keep walking, find a way out eventually and live happily ever after.

James' conclusion was that your action makes your belief true. However, I believe that it is the particular *belief* that creates the ensuing reality. It is your focused intent as well as your positive or negative vibration that creates your reality to shift either way.

The important thing to note is that whichever way that you look at it; in both scenarios you are the creators of your reality! You are constantly creating your reality whether you realise it or not.

We are affected by the Law of Attraction (LOA) all day every day and one of the major stumbling blocks to achieving a life of joy is ignorance of how this powerful law works.

Put quite simply LOA states that 'like attracts like'. You are a powerful magnet attracting experiences by the vibratory nature of your thoughts and feelings.

You get what you think and feel about a subject whether that be consciously or subconsciously. By this, I mean not just your conscious goals and intentions but also the deeply ingrained morals, values and belief programs that form the foundation of who you really are.

The LOA as presented by *Abraham has three basic stages:
(Abraham is the name given to a group of non-physical teachers that are channelled by Esther Hicks)

1. You ask – You are asking in a multitude of ways just by being alive and active. You also ask innately or perhaps subconsciously with your personal vibration. You also ask on a conscious level with direct focus, setting intentions, goals and clarifying your desires.

2. It is given – This is the universe's job and anything that you ask for is given immediately.

3. You must allow – This is the hardest part because you must be in a matching vibrational state to the thing that you are requesting, as well as in alignment with your soul energy for your wish to manifest.
Let us look at each of these stages more closely.

Stage 1: You ask
Your thoughts and feelings are actually made up of vibration and energy that can be recorded as a certain frequency by Electro Encephalography (EEG) machines. The brain's cells produce tiny electrical signals when they communicate with each other. These devices are now so sensitive that these signals can be recorded in the field around your head in a technique called Magneto Encephalography. Your thoughts and feelings are broadcasting constantly into the field around you.
I will not go deeply into the science here, but basically quantum physicists have proposed that the field of energy that surrounds us is the medium through which manifestation into matter is caused via the observation of a 'consciousness'. In simple terms:
"I think therefore I (create) matter!"
The act of asking is not really difficult in itself, but you should understand that it is important to be conscious of what it is that

you are asking for. You are creating and broadcasting desires consciously, subconsciously and emotionally. Therefore it is useful to remember that by sometimes experiencing things that you do not want you are more able to define exactly what you do want.

Stage 2: It is given

Atoms are referred to as the building blocks of life. Everything in physical existence is made from atoms including you, the chair that you are sitting on and this book. The physical form that all of those things have taken is due to the different vibration rate of those atoms. Everything in creation begins as a thought. That chair that you are sitting on was an idea in the designer's mind at some point that eventually became form through his focused attention.

How thoughts become form after focused attention in some ways then is pure physics. It is an automatic process and thus there are no judgements about your worth or level of deserving anywhere within that process.

If you have the ability to conceive of the idea then the universe has the ability to bring it to you. However, the field through which that manifestation comes is responding to your specific personal vibration on each subject and not just to your words and thoughts.

Stage 3: You must allow

You are broadcasting your thoughts and feelings to the universe and everyone around you every minute of every day through both the heart and mind fields. The things that match these vibrations and frequencies are the very things which you will find manifesting in the form of daily circumstances, events and people that surround you today.

I know that when I was severely depressed, for example, I had a lot of other people in my life that were negative and stressed that I now see matched my vibrational state. Like attracts like.

Think about your TV set. All of the possible programs are beamed from a transmitter station or satellite elsewhere through the field of airways and you can only receive the station to which your TV is tuned into. All the other possible stations exist and continue to be beamed, but because you are tuned into a station called BBC1, for example, you would be unable to receive any other channel unless you intentionally change your 'dial' and retune to the different frequency that ITV, for example, operates on. Note that you cannot receive two different channels at once.

We all can understand this concept and use it with the radio or television all our lives, I am sure. We never expect to press the button for BBC1 on our remote controls and get Channel 4 for example.

This is exactly how the LOA works. It is pure physics. It is absolutely reliable and works just the same as any other immutable law in the universe, such as gravity. So if science tells us that we are the conscious observer, affecting the field and thus the creator of our reality, it must then follow logically that all our requests should manifest. Pure physics, yes?

So where are my millions of pounds? Ah, if only life was that simple, eh? Well, in some ways it is. The process is simple but it is us as complex human beings that are the problem. However, if we are the problem then we are also the solution. So let us delve a little deeper into what is really going on here

Let us pause for a moment to look around our lives and see what is present. Whatever you see is exactly what you have been asking for consciously or unconsciously because LOA is a faithful servant! This is what you have allowed to manifest into your life.

Probably the first thing that we notice is that there are many things in our lives about which we could immediately declare, "I would not have wanted, chosen or created that!"

The painful truth though is that nothing turns up in your experience out of the blue. That would go against the very law by which you live your life. So the only other conclusion must be that you are oblivious to the vibration that you were broadcasting! You are receiving exactly what you are tuned into receive.

For example, if you are mainly tuned into anger, asking and visualizing for happiness will never net you the 'thing' that you want to bring you joy. In this instance, you will be most likely to attract lots of things that make you angry including the fact that the happiness has not turned up yet!

Not only this, but when your vibrational state is anger it will build momentum causing things to make you even more angry to turn up. This is why when things go wrong, the situation tends to spiral.

Conversely when you are 'on a roll' of winning, you seem to get luckier and luckier. We have that saying "money goes to money" for good reason. If you feel lucky and rich it is much easier to attract more riches and luck because your vibration is one of abundance.

I saw a really interesting documentary recently by the British illusionist Derren Brown about how we make our own luck. It highlighted LOA and how we are the creators of our own reality perfectly. For example, there was one man who believed he was unlucky and who was given many opportunities to win things – such as a winning scratch card put through his door and a street questionnaire especially designed so that he would answer it correctly and win £20. But the failed to see the opportunity of the winning card and said he was too busy to do the street questionnaire. The researchers even put £20 on the path in front of him and he still failed to spot it. Psychologists say that lucky people are those that see and act on every opportunity available. I would argue that these people have a belief program that says they are lucky and that this then manifests for them by the process of focused attention, observation and action. The difference is that believing is seeing rather than seeing is believing as most of us have been taught!

To try and demonstrate how this works from the LOA standpoint we will work with money because most people want more money. However, some people believe that money is at best, not spiritual and at worse evil. But that is just a limiting belief! Creation didn't say we are all one – except money; 'you are bad, you sit in the corner over there in shame, you naughty coloured rectangle of paper!' Everything is spiritual.

I like to think of money as how the trees go on holiday, travelling around the world and interacting with lots of different people and things.

I went on a course once with a guy who said that he would kiss every note that he spent and say "goodbye my friend, come back to me with all your children!" I thought that was a wonderful vibration to have around money, a sense of love and playfulness!

I have chosen money because it is a good way to show that we all have belief programs running that affect our success or failure around manifestation.

Let us imagine that Gina believes that she is generally happy about everything in her life and but decides that she wants more money and prays for a million pounds. She wants to give up the job that she is bored in, to have a nicer house and to be free to do what she wants to do when she want to do it.

In reality, it is not the nicer house that Gina wants, but the feeling that having a nicer house will give to her. Money itself will not bring her happiness but it is the tool that allows her to do things or have things that will make her *feel* happy.

On a side note, I would just like to bring to your attention some salient points about money. It seems to be that money is what most people, including me for a long time, feel is what they need to solve all their problems and make them happy. However, money is a benign tool, but it is how YOU handle it that's positive or negative. Money is power, money is choice and money can make you feel extremely secure and consequently happy. Money equals freedom and experiences.

Money has given you almost everything around you that is not natural. Money has already been very good to you!

Pause for a moment and think about something that you want in life. It could be an object, a relationship, or a different state. Now ask yourself: What would that give me? How would that make me feel?

You will always end up with the desire for happiness in whatever terminology you use. Like all life forms, we all just want to move away from pain and towards pleasure.

To ask and to want more is our natural state of being and it is life enhancing. It permits growth and on-going evolution. Remember that the universe is infinitely abundant. When you receive something from the universe you will not have received it due to the universe having removed it from anyone or anywhere else. Greed is impossible as long as you are not taking action that is physically taking or receiving something at another person's expense so there should be no guilt about wanting more.

The Dual Nature of All Subjects

We already know that everything is neutral until we judge it. When we judge, what we are actually doing is choosing to focus on one end of an object or subject that is dual in nature.

Take a pencil, for example. A pencil has two ends; if I look at the end with the lead in it then by inference I must also be aware that there is an end with the rubber on.

We discussed earlier with the example of words in a sentence, it is the space around something (that which it is not) that brings the object into form and defines the object. Thus the pencil is defined by the space in which ALL of it exists. By that very definition, I then have to become conscious of the two ends which form the boundary of where the pencil begins and ends in order to be able to identify that it is a pencil. You will remember about duality that everything has its opposite or complimentary state.

Every subject is really two subjects — that which is wanted and the lack of it. Thus if Gina says that she wants to be a millionaire, there is also her recognition that at this point in time she is not a millionaire.

What's more, every time she says that she wants to be a millionaire but feels the absence of the money in her everyday life, she is actually, unintentionally *reinforcing* the vibration of lack. Every time her heart sinks when she sees another bill to be paid or she thinks 'I can't afford that', she is restating the feeling that she is not a millionaire and consequently she is attracting more experiences of not being a millionaire.

If, however, Gina could find a way to feel wealthy for most of the day – by for instance, feeling grateful for the services that her money pays for - then she would instead activate the vibration of wealth and appreciation that would allow the million pounds to manifest

Let us pause for a moment and say:

'I am wealthy'.

Now let us spend a few moments looking around us and listing all the things that we appreciate such as good health, clean fresh water, the sunshine, our loved ones, our pets etc (Please notice that things to not have to cost anything in order to make us feel wealthy!)

Now again say again but this time with recognition of how truly wealthy we are

"Wow, I really am wealthy."

If by doing this exercise you have been able to achieve a feeling of wealth, you can start to understand what I mean here because the vibrational broadcast is very different when you truly feel and believe something.

I should add here that there is a big difference between the vibration of need and want. If Gina wants the money, but can maintain a happiness set point whether it turns up or not then she will be more likely to succeed in attracting the money.

If, however, the vibration is a deep need because her debts are increasing and she is struggling to pay her rent then she will be less likely to attract the money. One is a vibrational set point of abundance while the latter is a vibrational set point of poverty.

It is also important here to think about poverty consciousness in general. Poverty consciousness can be on any subject and is always about fear and lack.

I recently had an experience which showed me that I was actually moving away from this vibration of lack and fear. A friend of mine recently told me that she was training to be a hypnotherapist and I am proud to say that I did immediately everything that I could to help her. At the time, another friend said I was mad because my hypnotherapist friend was potentially my business rival as we live in the same area.

If I had bought into that belief, which end of the pencil would I be focused on—abundance or lack? Luckily for me, I am confident in my skills, already established and had already moved into the belief program that says I create my reality. I could therefore help her from a place of abundance.

Chapter 7: LOA and the Two of You

"The thankful heart is always closest to the riches of the Universe" Mahatma Gandhi

Firstly let me reaffirm that a vibration and the field are completely non-judgemental. Your TV set does not say 'I am not showing 'Friends' tonight because you shouted at your child this morning' or 'you do not do enough charity work!' If you can press the right button on the remote control and thus tune the set there it must manifest - it is the law!

In the last chapter we have seen how duality works in one way with the LOA, but there is also another relationship of duality that we must consider in this work.

Abraham describes how your manifestations are actually affected by your relationship with what 'they' describe as 'Source' and which for them means the nonphysical 'part' of you. In their analogy, they explain that there are not two separate parts of you-one physical and one nonphysical (one alive and one 'dead' if you like) but that the physical you is in fact an extension of Source energy.

One of my first moves out of the corporate world was by training as a Reiki therapist. Reiki, as you may know, is a form of energy healing. In the attunement ceremony that opens you up to the working with Reiki, I had a deeply emotional experience whereby on asking to meet my guide I was shown an enormous but beautiful ship's figurehead. She was a rosy cheeked, glorious woman whose name was offered as Mahatma. This in itself surprised me because I had always associated Mahatma with Gandhi and as such believed this to be a man's name.

To be honest, I had always been a little sceptical about guides and angels, but the unusualness of the name meant that I could be sure that I would not have made this up consciously. I really did not understand the connotations to begin with, but I later realized that a ship's figurehead guides and protects the ship on its journey - just as my lovely guide has watched over mine (Thank you Mahatma)

However, about a year ago I discovered that in Buddhism there exists a term Mahatmya which is the expression of the greater self or universal soul.

I also found that Mahatmya is translated as 'Big Self' or Divine Goddess in the Vedic tradition. I was absolutely amazed as I definitely had never heard of this name or idol before and certainly not all those years ago when I completed my Reiki attunement and met my 'Big Self' for the first time.

I now understand that Mahatmya is actually my eternal soul energy or Source in Abraham speak. Mahatmya, I believe, is the non-physical source that provides the electricity or energy that operates the biological quantum super-computer which is me in my physical form.

I also believe that she is inextricably linked to and communicates with my Higher Self via my right brain hemisphere and heart.

Let us further explore this through the analogy of the computer and its electrical power source.

Without the computer, for example, any electricity in your home would flow towards the house, but would be unfocused and essentially pointless. Yet without the electricity source and the computer plugged into the energy, the computer itself is in some ways pointless. The two must be inextricably linked if either is to have any meaningful purpose. This is analogous to the non-physical and the physical you. The two parts have to work together in a physical environment. They are two, the Yin and Yang, of the operating system of my life.

Thus you need to take into account both parts of 'you' in order to have any meaningful outcomes with the Law of Attraction.

It is your in-house emotional guidance system that is responsible for just that. It informs you constantly where both parts of the system are in relationship to each other and aims to guide the physical you towards the much needed energy of your soul.

I find that this is the part of the work that most people miss the significance of, as I also did for many years.

Abraham uses the analogy of a satellite navigation system. Just like a traditional satellite navigation system in your car, the emotional guidance system will always show you faithfully where you currently are on the screen. In the same way you are also constantly being shown where you are physically in relation to your goal and greatness.

Ok, going back to my earlier example, let us say that Gina is very frustrated that her million pounds has still not manifested. Most of us have been taught to believe that the frustration we are experiencing is merely an emotion, just something that is and mostly we experience it without question. We must now understand, however, that what that feeling really is trying to tell us is that the source part of us (the non-physical) is feeling something very different to the physical part (frustration). To the source abundance and wealth is our birth right. Consequently, it is telling Gina that she is out of alignment with the feeling that she needs to have in order to manifest the money.

Or to use the Sat-nav analogy: Gina has programmed in that she is here in London, and her destination is Millionaires-Ville.

The system is telling her through the emotion of frustration that she needs to change direction. It is telling her that she cannot get to Millionaires-Ville from there doing, feeling and thinking what she is currently doing, thinking and feeling! She is going the wrong way about it!

Again just to drive home (excuse the pun!) this really important point, please allow me to me present this is in a more visual if a little lyrical way.

As Mahatmya lives outside of the limitations of this 'physical' reality, she is already living the millionaire's lifestyle. Not physically obviously, but through the essence of the vibration of being a millionaire which is abundance and deep joy. 'We' asked and it was immediately given. Because she has no resistance, no old programs running, no limiting beliefs etc she has allowed the vibration of abundance to 'manifest' immediately.

Mahatmya is pure vibration, always joyous and always blissful (especially now she is a millionaire!!!) But seriously...

Because I exist in what I believe to be a physical environment with limitations and old and contrary belief programs running, I am the only thing that is actually preventing my money from being delivered by the big postman in the sky. He is waiting patiently outside my door ringing the bell but I can't hear it. This is because I am shouting out so loudly in frustration that I have waited so long. I mistakenly believe that the Post Office has obviously lost my cheque!

Although the feeling of bliss, which should be my natural state of being, is missing, I remain inextricably linked to the part of me that is always feeling that bliss. Thus when I feel really bad, it is that I am *really* experiencing the desire to get back to my natural state of bliss. Or in other words, I have gone off track.

Any negative emotion is really a manifestation of the little me out of alignment with the soul energy me. The computer is too far away from the electricity supply if you like. We discussed emotions being about power in previous chapters. I am really experiencing a shortage of soul energy which leaves me feeling less powerful than I know that I really am. I am Mahatmya. I am a creator and thus when I act as if I am not that or at least equal to that then I am denying my true power. And this is what the frustration is drawing my attention to.

The key to success is to work to maintain a state of joy so that my *foundation* vibrational state is joy. Then the only thing that could manifest for me are things that match the vibration of joy. My work is then to develop a belief that I am a powerful creator *solely* responsible for creating my world and to reinforce it with all of my thoughts, feelings and actions. If I can keep focused on that and remove any opposing programs that counteract the first belief then I am clear to manifest anything, simply by paying constant attention to my feelings. Ultimately, our sole focus should be on moving towards the next exciting thing, and then the next one, and then the one after that…

So how can I manifest those things that I desire?

Some Tools for Creation

Now let us quickly run through some of the tools that aid in manifestation.

There are many games and tools which will help you to achieve manifestations through the LOA. Visualisation, affirmations and meditation are three of the most powerful as you are giving clear, focused attention to your goal.

Firstly, affirmations are not airy fairy rote phrases or wishful thinking. As you will see in the chapter Brain vs. Mind, repetition of an affirmation is a powerful way to program the mind or to create a new pathway in the brain. The repetition of the affirmation is the propellant that takes you forward on the new journey. A belief is a thought that you keep thinking and thus to keep thinking the new positive thought ensures that it becomes your new belief, your new truth, which will be reinforced by your reality!

"I think therefore I (create) matter and so it matters what I think" is thus a powerful, positive and multi layered affirmation. However, remember that it is not just about your thoughts but it is also about your feeling and vibration. Affirmations therefore, should be powerful, positive and stated in the present tense.

With visualisation and meditation you are also working with the awesome power of the imagination and subconscious mind together. By using all the senses possible and visualising yourself in the moment, celebrating your success and really feeling all the attendant emotions of joy and excitement, it becomes extremely powerful. In meditation the resistant thoughts will slowly become dormant.

It has been suggested that the brain knows no difference between what it imagines to be real and what it is seeing in reality. The same areas light up under a MRI scanner in both scenarios. So if you can hold the attention strongly enough for long enough the object of your desire should manifest.

Vision boards are a powerful tool to aid manifestation. A vision board is a board on which you place pictures, words or drawings of the things that you wish to attract into your life.

The idea is that you focus on the boards every day and practice the feeling of having those things or living that life as if you had them now.

I had a strange experience where I read a book called 'Autobiography of a Yogi' in 2012 and it mentioned an extremely powerful non-physical teacher, a Mahavatar called Babaji, and showed a picture of 'him' in the book. I had never seen or heard of Babaji before but for some reason the striking image of 'him' stayed in my mind. The next morning after my meditation, I looked over to my left-hand side where I had recently moved an old vision board to and was amazed to see a tiny picture of Babaji on it. I don't remember consciously ever seeing it before, yet alone knowing why I would have put it on there. I can only think that I did that to fill in a small gap on the board.

So in 2007 - five years before I came to even know of this teacher I had placed an image of him on my vision board for the future.

I suddenly realised that I was not creating boards of wishes for the future, but my future was being shown to me on the boards.

I felt that in 2007 that I was showing myself that this would occur in the future. It is a very small and subtle nuance but it fits perfectly with the idea that all things exist simultaneously in this moment now - past, present and future at once. All of that knowledge is already accessible to me now and so those boards are akin to me spelling out to me what I believe my most probable future will be. It is only the most probable future outcomes from where I am now because I always have free will to change my mind at any point along the way.

I was blown away by this because it took away all the uncertainty and really focused my belief that whatever is on that board - if I still want it - is destined to appear.

Thus I decided to create a new belief program in that moment that there is nothing to worry about. All I need to do is keep watching out for the inspired action that I need to take in order to keep myself moving on the same path.

Another tool that Abraham gives us to deal with stopping unwanted momentum and allowing us to become aware of our vibration is segment intending. As an aside, I used this to good effect when I had one very stressful area of my life but I still had to function normally in the others. Basically, you must try to consciously stop at every new segment or scene change in your life. You then decide what you *want* to create next. In this way you will be more able to ensure that the negative vibration of the stressful situation doesn't creep into the next situation or overtake any other part of the day.

Thus I would come away from the stress and say ok now I am at work, now I am lunch, now I am…. and separate the different parts of my life so that one did not overtake the others. I felt very in control and empowered by this. In this way I could keep a high flying vibration despite the conditions of that current reality.

Another interesting exercise to uncover hidden beliefs and programs is to create a mind map. My favourite way to create a mind map is to write on one side of the paper any positive phrases that come to mind about a subject - without judgement - and on the other side the negative phrases. You can do the negative phrases in different coloured ink for emphasis. It will soon become clear visually if the subject is a negative or positive in your view. It is then your job to start releasing or amending those belief programs that you do not want. This is an interesting exercise because you will come up with lots of proverbs or catchphrases that you may have collected from society without even thinking about whether they are true or not for you personally. For example: 'Money is the root of all evil'. Really, is that true for you?

If you are resistant or do not have the time to do mind mapping, another of Abraham's techniques is to write a list of positive aspects about whatever subject that you are having trouble with. This contains everything that you can think of that is positive, or you are grateful or appreciate about *that* thing at least once a day.

I find this a really good thing to do if I have already discovered why I am creating a situation but I am still working on embedding the new programming. Whilst I am having a few minor irritations with a person, situation or 'thing' in my life it is a very quick way to change my vibration about them in that moment.

In conclusion then, the LOA is a powerful law that we must take into account if we are truly going to take full responsibility for creating our own reality. Having trust and faith in that is the key to happiness. Living in the moment, unconditionally accepting that everything is meant to be and feeling genuine excitement about the next thing and the next thing is an amazingly freeing and empowering way to live your life.

Try it because believing is seeing!

But what if I am not seeing all those things that I say that I want? Let us now deal with the main problem for most people-non manifestation!

Chapter 8: LOA – Non-Manifestation

"If you think you can or you think you can't, either way you are right" Henry Ford

Let us now look at why non manifestation and misalignment happens and how to remedy it. You may recognize these programs as blocks and negative belief programs.

It is important to take ownership of the lack of manifestation. Remember *you* are always the problem. This work requires that you take full and unconditional responsibility for everything. So you must now look at what you would have to really believe in order to manifest the lack of the money, for example. If this is the reality that is manifesting, it must be because there is a stronger belief program running than the one which you say that you want - the million pounds. This must be true because when you ask it is always given, but it is the strongest belief and the current vibration that will absolutely manifest first.

Going back to Gina, we recall that she has asked for a million pounds but it has not turned up and she has started to doubt that the LOA works. Inside her subconscious or underneath her conscious thoughts, Gina may have a program of fear running that goes like this: If I became a Millionaire:
How would I keep my old friends? Where would I move too? Would I be targeted by burglars if I lived in a big house? What would happen if I then lost it all? I do not deserve it etc. These latter two statements are, I believe, major belief programs that affect many of us subconsciously regarding wealth in particular!

The TOUR worksheets that we will look at later are designed to help you to uncover the underlying beliefs and programs. However, there are other reasons why her manifestations may not appear.

It could be that the non-receipt of money may actually be the best thing for Gina because it will force her to really find out what programs are going on in her mind so that she can clear them and live a happier life with or without the money. There can be more to gain in the overall success of life if we can accept that success is based on the evolution of the soul. If we measure success in this way, we can also understand that the desire for money is just a tool that Gina is using to discover more about herself and to clear some of the underlying beliefs hidden in her shadows.

I have come to understand that I at least, now use the LOA as a journey of self-discovery rather than as a tool for manifestation. I only complete self-reflection work when there is a non-manifestation or a problem and so I create problems in order to continue to do the work that I believe ultimately is the point of my whole life – the evolution of my consciousness!

I had been asking for a large amount of money until recently. However, I then noticed that I had received something far more valuable in my life by NOT receiving it. If I had been able to manifest a large amount of money when I was younger, I would have brought a house, a car and gone and lay on a beach somewhere. My life would have taken a very different direction to the one that it has and I would be oblivious to all the fears and negative belief programs that I had running. In view of this I do not think that the wealth and happiness would have lasted very long.

When I first uncovered the gain that the *non-manifestation* had brought me, I realised that I would not have changed that for the world let alone a million pounds. All of the work that I have done, the learning, the evolution and the people that I have helped as a consequence of having to keep looking for the reason my manifestations sometimes would not come has for me been invaluable. It has been a true gift that has actually brought me the happiness that I was originally looking for through the money. How amazing is that?

So although Gina may believe that she needs the money to be happy, with all those underlying blocks and fears that we previously mentioned, we could say that subconsciously she does not really want the money. These are actually opposing vibrations and so there will be a tug of war vibration occurring that says yes-no-yes-no. She will feel like she is stuck in life.

In the teachings of Abraham, there is now an analogy about laying new pipes. This is a reference to the fact that if your pipes are clogged and nothing is moving through them it is a good idea to get off that particular subject. In this scenario, this may look like giving up the tug of war and just concentrating on feeling appreciation for everything that you do have. If you are really feeling a deep need or frustration around a non-manifestation then to keep trying to focus on it will just keep churning up the blocks and re-clogging the pipes. Unless this is actually the work that you want to do in order to have the opportunity to clear programs then you would be better off avoiding the subject or laying new pipes.

What this means is focusing your attention on looking for something to make you happy in every moment of every day on any other subject. If you are only interested in manifestations as opposed to self-discovery then this option is definitely the easiest route.

I have found the best way to feel wealthy and happy is to be grateful every waking moment for everything that you are and that you have. Every person has something to be grateful for even if it is just the fact that they are alive.

If tomorrow you were told that you were terminally ill, you would probably have a sudden desperation to fight and beat the disease and to stay alive. It must follow then that life must be worth living and so be grateful that you are here and hopefully mainly healthy.

It is good to remember that the very things that are most valuable are those given freely: sunshine, rain, fresh air, health, water, nature, beauty and love etc. Waking up every morning and noticing how wealthy you already are will allow whatever you want to manifest more easily because that is where your most practised vibration will be.

It is important to remember that anything you are asking for is only a tool to fulfil your real wish which is to be happy or to feel good! That is really what the million pounds would bring you. At the end of the day, if you have enough money to do what you need to do, when you need to do it then you are already rich. You do not need to have all your Christmas dinners in one day. We trust that every year we will be able to manifest the Christmas dinner every year on cue - and so it is.

So use whatever you can to hold the intention to feel good every moment of every day. Trust that as the creator of your Universe, you will deliver the money, the partner and the house then let it go. Have faith and believe that it has already been given. If you order something from mail order, for example, you do not keep ringing up asking "did you get my order, did you get my order…when is it coming, when is it coming?"

You have to trust in the system. This makes manifestation easier and less susceptible to the counter effect of opposing, negative belief programs. Lack of trust is one way in which we fail to manifest exactly what we desire, the other is through impatience.

Think about a seed that you have planted into the ground that takes three weeks before it grows into a shoot. If you planted the seed without this knowledge, you may have given up hope after two weeks when nothing was showing above ground. You may come to the mistaken conclusion that nothing was going to happen. You may stop watering the seed or even dig up the ground and start again.

Sometimes our manifestations come at the time that is right for us – as judged by our soul perhaps in light of our larger themes. The soul sees the world very differently from us and is not concerned with our trivial wants and needs.

There is a saying that God always answers prayers in one of three ways:

'Yes', 'not yet' or 'I've got something better planned!'

It is important to have faith and that includes faith even if - for reasons that we do not immediately understand - our hearts' desire fails to manifest how and when that we think it should.

Often that is exactly what we do with our goals and intentions. If I do not see it manifest immediately, my attention wanders and I think that LOA does not work but there are often signs of shoots appearing that we do not see.

For example, if I were to travel from London to Glasgow then I would not expect to see road signs for Glasgow which is 400 miles away as soon as I left home. The sign for the A1 is enough to tell me that I am heading in the right direction. However, if I did not know that I needed to go on the A1 first, I may panic at not seeing any signs for Glasgow and give up. It would only be when I was a few miles away that I would see a sign stating Glasgow. But it is still a fact that I was on track to 'manifest' Glasgow perfectly because I had been given signs that affirmed that it was coming for the last 390 odd miles.

LOA is the same. The clues that my millions are about to appear might arrive in less obvious ways – a small win on the lottery perhaps or an unexpected pay rise at work, for example. Your wish may manifest in a most unexpected way.

In one of my classes, a student talked about wanting a new car, but not being able to afford one. A few weeks later, her husband was unexpectedly left some money in a will and so they suddenly had the money for a new car. Now if the student had spent time and effort focused on winning the lottery in order to buy the car, she would have actually been shutting the door on the possibility of the money coming from somewhere else.

We sometimes forget that this is an extremely intricately designed, intelligent Universe and do it a great dishonour by thinking that we know the only or best way for things to manifest. After putting the request for the car out there, the best thing for the woman to do was to trust the Universe to find a way to get it to her! Your manifestations come through the path of least resistance. That really means the easiest way that the

Universe can start to get things through to you. It is crucial then for you to find a way to feel happy with or without the manifestations, otherwise you are living conditional love as such. The limiting belief program of 'I can only be happy *if or when* something appears' will keep you stuck forever!

Impatience is not a bad thing as such because it shows a deep wanting, but the letting go of the need is vitally important because, as Albert Einstein said, "nature abhors a vacuum". Thus if you can spend what money you do have, it makes room for the new to manifest as you are telling the Universe that you already have it to give. In addition, the spending of money makes you feel wealthy and as if you are, indeed, moving up the emotional scale in the right direction.

The Emotional Scale

The emotional scale is in some ways linked to the guidance system. It directs us always towards the next positive emotion on it. If we say desperation or depression may lie at the end of the pencil with the rubber on and extreme bliss on the lead end then our emotions are somewhere in between. It is your job to keep finding something to focus on that will get you step by step up to the lead end. You have to move along the pencil gradually though, you cannot jump through the whole emotional scale in one go. It is impossible to be depressed in one minute and truly blissful the next. You must focus on feeling a little bit happier each day to reach true bliss.

When I was developing the TOUR tool, I had that epiphany. I started working through the TOUR to check it works for every subject. When things are going well for me, which thankfully is 99.9% of the time now, I am grateful and appreciative but I never really search for the programs and beliefs that underline that. It is only the occasional minor irritations that make me do some work. My epiphany was that I realised that I will always need to have something 'negative' in my life to work on. Wow! This caused a sudden shift in me and it was then I understood that I could keep my focus just on all the positive things with which to do my work.

One aspect of the Law of Attraction is that we need the contrast of any particular emotional state or event in order to see clearly what it is that we do want. That may mean having minor irritations occur because having more of 'what it is not' creates an opportunity for negativity as contrast to make you focus on what you do want more of. Contrast is a positive thing because it allows what we do want to stand out from the background.

The shift is to understand that we need to uncover the negative subconscious programs, but that we also need to reinforce the positive ones that are making those parts of our lives successful. To focus on these positive beliefs and programs produces more manifestations because it continually reinforces our strengths and successes. Therefore, find an area of your life that is working well and 'model' or transfer those same qualities or skills over to the areas that are not doing so well for you.

So for me, an area of success is work and as such is therefore my path of least resistance as far as money is concerned. I can get almost anything that I want to manifest quickly and easily without any problem at all - except large amounts of *unearned* money.

I can earn money easily so although I may not win a large sum of money, I can build my wealth gradually through work. I have strong programming and beliefs about the moral value and my self-esteem coming from working that was ingrained in childhood. In some way it is a good program.

Through the constant questioning of which programs I have running that may be keeping large windfalls of money away, I have discovered a whole host of other beliefs and programs about who and what I am. Win - win again. I have been constantly peeling away the layers of my onion of beliefs that have made the rest of my life bliss.

I know that I have been given an opportunity to really define who I am. I am learning who I want to be *through* my journey. Thus, I help others by sharing *my* knowledge! My next book will be entitled 'How Not to Win the Lottery!'

In some ways then it is the arguing with reality that causes our suffering. Feeling frustrated because the millions did not arrive today is arguing with reality while accepting that we are healthy and wealthy in other ways allows the flow of wellbeing and abundance to come into our lives. That is why I consider LOA to be whole life living and not just something that you concentrate on now and again. Yes, we can work on specific things, but we have various core beliefs and values and an emotional set point from which we mainly manifest. It is paying constant attention to feeling good in every moment, on every subject and not allowing others to affect our vibration that I feel is vital.

Momentum

When I decided to write this book, I talked about it constantly. I laughingly call it my new best seller not because I am arrogant but because I now understand that I need to 'act as if' it already is a success, in order to create the right *vibrational* state and to build up the *momentum* of success.

Discussing your worries and constantly talking about how scared you are of the exam or interview coming up, for example, will build momentum and put you on the path of failure quicker than anything else. It is almost like you are asking the universe to grant your wish of failure! When you make a request or statement, it helps to imagine a big genie in the sky waving a wand and granting that wish!

People are often very self-deprecating but if you do not believe in yourself as a success then who else will? If you cannot muster a feeling inside of you around success then how can you hope to live that out?

When I teach students about the Law of Attraction, I always encourage them to spend a lot of time celebrating what they did well each day. If they receive a compliment, I encourage them to go over and over it in their mind, continually deepening their positive self-esteem and self-love. Doing this alone will keep you focused on the positive end of the pencil.

In Britain particularly, we do not allow people to shine. Think about how our press, for example, spend so much time destroying celebrities or successful people. Remember that everyone who is successful, even the celebrity, is really the successful part of you that wants to shine. They may cause negative reactions from you to show you that you are not living your glory. It is the contrast that forces you to look at you. However, you may have programming that subconsciously warns against it. The destruction in your reality of the celebrity then begins showing you what you subconsciously think will happen to you if you dared to shine.

We definitely do not want to hear about anyone else telling us how fabulous they are. We call that arrogance. I have programming from childhood about being called a 'big head' by siblings if I had any success. I quickly learned that if I wanted to be liked then I needed to keep my head under the parapet.

This has affected my programming amongst other things about winning, standing out from a crowd and following society's 'rules'.

Wow with that programming I am lucky to have achieved anything in life!

It has taken me years to uncover all of these programs and their influences on my behaviour and goals. But I now realize that these are just programs that I can remove. So if you are finding any discomfort with my suggestion that you start to own your magnificence, then I suggest that you use the TOUR worksheet to start unpicking the reasons very quickly!

Whilst you are uncovering those beliefs I want you to accept that you are allowed to celebrate yourself - to yourself. I am not advocating going around shouting from the roof tops or telling everyone you meet that you are fabulous. But I do advise you to remind yourself that it is special to be you and to own all of the good qualities, joys and successes that make up that the wonder that is you. Build your own momentum of success.

Creating and Reviewing the Day

One of my favourite ways to reflect on and build momentum and positive vibration is to create my day in the morning and to review it in the evening. I connect these two things with my meditation time so it has become part of my routine.

In the morning, I create my day by seeing and knowing that every detail will play out exactly as I visualise it. I visualise and feel gratitude for the free parking spaces, the quick and easy job being completed or the meeting going well. I know and trust that all of my requests have already been granted.

Remember "I think therefore I (create) matter and so it matters what I think"

Then at the end of the day, I look for all the things that did manifest and celebrate them fervently. If something has not manifested then I just focus on what did work so that I can keep the vibration and momentum of success.

Now like anything that you wish to create, it is all a matter of belief. If to start with you do not really believe that this is possible then it may not manifest immediately, if at all. Trust that everything is being taken care of perfectly including the timings and you will find peace. If you start to watch closely during your review of the day and remain focused on what did manifest perfectly then more success must come.

The more you build up your momentum of belief the more you will create with confidence and the more you will see manifesting which in turn strengthens the belief. Repetition, as you will see later, deepens the pathway in the brain until it becomes the program and pathway of choice! Knowledge is power and just like the mechanic who knows immediately what is wrong with his car and so has no fear, you too must know and understand yourself fully so that you do not need to fear any problems.

I cannot stress enough that it is vital to stay consciously awake and only focus on those things that did manifest and really feel the empowerment and excitement of that. Remember that you cannot have a nightmare unless you are asleep! It is the believing that allows us to see. So the review of the day is really how and when you do your best work of creation and raise yourself to those higher vibrations by celebrating your success.

You must be the person that is constantly aware, constantly self-reflective and looking all the time for the things that make you feel good. It is the torch in the dark room scenario - you can decide to shine your torch and illuminate the scary doll in one corner or focus it on the beautiful laughing baby in the other. It is possible to become dedicated to taking your attention away from anything negative if you set an intention to do so. You will know what those things are, by paying attention to how anything feels in the moment. By inference then it is also possible to constantly hold your attention on to anything positive or at least distract yourself from that which is not. You simply need to follow your joy and excitement.

An inspirational teacher, coach or someone you may want to role model will always be able to lead or guide you to the success that already exists within you as buried treasure, but it is *you* that must do the actual digging.

Of course, being in the presence of someone that is living in a very high vibrational frequency like The Dalai Lama will uplift you! Then you, as an aspect of the teacher, will be more able to raise your vibration (if that is what you desire). If not, you will find that they are annoying to you and thus you will drop out of their life and awareness. This is why when you take the spiritual path of transformation some of your old acquaintances tend to disappear and a new circle of friends emerges. The vibrational difference is too great to sustain.

My job as a teacher and coach is to keep my vibration as high as I can in order to bring my clients and students up to me. If I lower my vibration in order to make them feel more comfortable then we both suffer.

In conclusion then, the LOA is a powerful law that we must take into account if we are truly going to take full responsibility for creating our own reality.

Your thoughts, your feelings and your goals all need to have your full and undivided attention. It is imperative that you stay awake and conscious of your thoughts and feelings.

Having trust and faith in the law is the key to happiness. Living in the moment, unconditionally accepting that everything is meant to be and feeling genuine excitement about the next thing and the next thing is an amazingly freeing and empowering way to live your life.

Try it because believing is seeing!

Chapter 9: The Brain vs Mind

"...ho is seriously involved in the pursuit of science
...nced that a spirit is manifest in the laws of the
...irit vastly superior to that of man." Albert Einstein

Researchers have long made a distinction between the brain and the mind. One researcher, Karl Pribham, investigated this division by systematically cutting away different sections of a rat's brain to try to discover where the memory was held. He was never able to locate its exact location and it is now proposed that memory must be located throughout the brain. Newer thinking, however, suggests that memory and consciousness may exist in 'fields' that surround us.

We have already established that we experience the world via our five senses. The discipline of Neuro-linguistic Programming (NLP) supports this theory, but adds that consciously and subconsciously we continuously delete, distort and filter any data that we do not want or need to pay attention to.

Thus, we create the world that we want or expect to see that matches our *particular* belief system.

Anais Nin deftly points out that "Often we do not see the world as it is but as we are!"

Neuroscientists tell us that the brain builds up nets or webs of associated information and experiences and then matches reality against its pre stored patterns. The more often that a net is accessed the more likely that it will become the pathway of choice. Just like on your computer, the program that you use the most will appear top of the menu list.

Let us say that the brain is the computer hardware and the mind is like the software. The internet, for example, like our thoughts does not exist within the computer itself. In the same way that you cannot access the internet without a computer or some form of hardware, as a physical human being, you cannot express consciousness without a functioning brain.

Sigmund Freud, the grandfather of psychoanalysis, proposed that behaviour and personality derive from the continuous ebb and flow of interactions between the three levels of awareness or the mind. He termed these levels: the preconscious, the conscious, and the unconscious.

He argued that the conscious mind included everything that we are consciously aware of in our day to day lives. We may think about this as the aspect of our mental processing that deals with rationality and logic.

The preconscious mind deals with our memory, while the unconscious mind is the remaining reservoir of feelings, thoughts, character traits and memories that are outside of and inaccessible to our immediate conscious awareness.

Freud compared these three levels of mind to an iceberg. His analogy was that the conscious mind is the tip of the iceberg that can be seen above the water, the preconscious mind is the part of the iceberg which is submerged below the water but still visible below the water line, and the unconscious mind is the remainder of the iceberg which is completely below the water line. Using this analogy, he proposed that the conscious mind was 5% of the total mind, the preconscious mind was 2% and the remaining 93% was the unconscious mind.

Many of the traits and qualities we have that we deem unacceptable or unpleasant are hidden in this unconscious beneath the 'water line'. Freud's theory is that the things within the unconscious continually try to influence our behaviour and experience. We are oblivious to this, but eventually get to see them in our everyday experience when we have projected them on to the other people or events in our lives. This is analogous to the Shadow that Carl Jung describes and which we discussed earlier in chapter entitled The Reality Mirror.

From Freud's iceberg analogy, we can see that the majority of our thoughts, beliefs and programs operate from below the level of our consciousness. This explains why it can often feel like everything is out of our control, that life happens to us and that we are powerless to change it. This is definitely not true, however. We feel like we are powerless because the fact that we are projecting out our issues was previously unconscious or unknown to us. But with enlightenment we become aware that we have a choice point at which to stop the automatic responses and at which instead to create a change.

I like this analogy: We are all carrying around a huge rucksack of stones that we do not even know is there. Even though the stones keep falling out and tripping us up, we still wonder where they are coming from. Sometimes we often pick them up and put them back in our rucksack.

Buddha said "The path is clear. Which rocks do you throw before you?" and it always reminds me of this scenario although that was not his intended meaning. It is only when we discover that the stones are falling out of our rucksack that we can start kicking them out of the way for good or at least be aware of them on our path.

The Choice Point

The choice point is the moment in which we become the deliberate selector of that next thought and can make the right choice of responding in a positive way as opposed to automatically reacting in a negative way.

In my classes, I like to use this simple analogy for how the mind programs. Suppose I have a mud path from my front door to my garden gate and that this is the most obvious route out of my property. Because it is a mud path, I have made a very deep rut in the mud by its continual use. (Let's say this is representative of the habitual or unquestioned, negative programs running in my mind). We shall call this the 'pathway of negative thinking'.

If I suddenly realise that I can actually choose to ride my bike across the lawn to leave the property and opt do this then soon I will have worn away the grass and made a pathway or rut in the ground there. This is the new belief or program of practised 'positive thinking.' If I continue to avoid using the mud path then eventually with the wind and rain, the mud will displace itself into the rut and the rut will eventually disappear.

In the same way, negative habitual programs cease to run after they are replaced by new positive programming. Remember, use it or lose it!

But in order to escape automatically going down the mud path to the gate as usual, I have to initially make a conscious decision or intention to change. I must also be attentive and aware so that before I even open my door, I know that I will have to aim for the grass. Making a resolution to change is easy, but the most important part is the action of peddling across the grass!

What's more, we need to keep peddling across the grass in order to keep that rut open. As we said earlier, positivity is a muscle that needs working out every day. This is the most important part of the process, but is the very thing that most of us fail to do.

The problem is that when you are in an emotional state, it is akin to the thoughts running with the brakes off. You will remember the IHM research that found that emotional processes can work faster than the mind. Thus, if you can ease your emotional state, clarity of thought in the moment becomes easier.

How can you do this? One useful tool which is increasing in popularity is mindfulness. Mindfulness is the awareness that emerges through deliberately paying attention to being in the present moment and accepting the reality of what is occurring in that moment. Being mindful in a situation allows you to slow the process, break the emotional state and then make a more considered and conscious choice.

Mindfulness in relation to this work is really about the awareness that comes from paying conscious attention, slowing down our thinking and then creating a gap that enables a response as opposed to a reaction. It allows you to enter the choice point and respond in a more positive or assertive way. In some ways, it is about being different as opposed to doing the same old thing.

I think we have all experienced this when after a row or argument and you chew it over hours later you start to realise there were things that it would have been better not to say or perhaps things that you felt that should have said. We may ask ourselves why we keep making the same old mistakes. It is because we are reacting emotionally.

Furthermore we react most often than not in habitual ways.

The sequence below shows how the thought process works.

Cycles of the Mind

1.   Observation/ Feedback
Real life example: 'No-one is serving me at the counter'

2.   Emotional response
'This makes me angry'

3.   Filter of beliefs then creates thought
'Everyone ignores me because I am weak'

4.   Now you've reached the Choice point for a positive response, e.g.
'I will make the point politely and firmly that I am next in the queue'

   Or Negative reaction: 'Start shouting abuse at the staff'

5.   Vibrational response will therefore be one of empowerment or more anger.

6.   Cycle begins again at this emotional set point and thus will play out more of the same.

Therefore the vibrational response creates the next positive or negative action, thought or emotion which will again reinforce empowerment or anger!

Please note: I have put the emotional response above the filtering of belief because although it may appear that the thought and emotion comes along together, it is the heart field that is taking in information before the brain. Thus the importance of being aware and consciously choosing your response rather than reaction is paramount.

If we look at the cycle, we see that there is an event or situation which we observe and receive feedback from. The person that we will call Jane is being ignored at the counter. This situation causes an emotional reaction. Jane experiences an emotion which triggers a vibrational state.

If at this point Jane feels and labels that sensation with the judgement of anger then that is what she will attract more of as the scenario plays out, both her anger and that of the assistant too.

As Buddha advises us "You will not be punished for your anger, you will be punished by your anger"

In the scenario, Jane has been ignored at the counter and she has now stimulated a raft of beliefs that already exist —one being that she is always ignored because she is weak. Obviously attached to this belief is an underlying network of associated beliefs and programs about not being good enough, being rejected etc. The brain forms neuro-nets of experiences, large webs of associated experiences, thoughts and beliefs that get linked together. For example, to recognize an apple, a picture of an apple doesn't exist in your memory bank as such.

The idea of an apple is 'layered' together from shape, size, taste, texture etc. This could be a simple neuro-net. However, if the teacher threw an apple at your head for chatting in class and that caused you great humiliation your neuro-net will now have teachers, classrooms and humiliation entangled within the mix of apple associations!

So Jane has labelled her emotion as anger and associated it with beliefs about weakness. Here is the work that I am advocating. It is important to be self-aware enough to intercept at the choice point and choose a conscious positive response as opposed to an automatic negative reaction.

If Jane is self-aware, she could recognise that the Universe is giving her through this situation, an opportunity to practice being assertive, which is one of her development goals. In this case, Jane would accept the invite and politely but firmly say to the clerk, "Excuse me but I am next to be served".

By responding in this way, Jane has taken her power back which will raise not only her self-esteem but also her vibration. It may also result in allowing her to get served. Even if her words provoked anger in the clerk, Jane still has a choice about whether to respond positively or react negatively. In every moment, we must take responsibility for our choices.

We have already discussed the fact that we cannot control or manage anyone else out there and nor do we need to. The clerk may just be having a bad day, be stressed or even short sighted. She genuinely may not have seen the customer and not even be aware that there was a problem. The point here is that how can we ever know what is really going on with another and what business is it of ours anyway?

Jane's only concern should be about what she is doing and taking full responsibility for her choices.

Whenever we believe people should act a certain way or treat us, as we deem to be fair, then we set ourselves up for suffering when it doesn't turn out the way that we are judging it should. Believing the false premise that life should be fair is one of the biggest causes of suffering that I see.

Your world, is made up of your programs which are either consciously known to you or dwelling in the recesses of your subconscious. These subconscious programs can become known by observing the people, relationships and occurrences in your life. These aspects continuously give you the opportunity to interact with those programs in order to heal, accept or practice a new behaviour.

Our emotions sometimes can be so automatic and unobserved that it will feel as though we are powerless to control them, but we know this is not true. What we need to do is to slow ourselves down. We can then give ourselves an opportunity to catch the choice point and to make better decisions. From the choice point, you can create the reality that you *choose* to consciously live rather than the reality that you believe is happening to you!

What actually causes the initial problem for Jane in the scenario above is her perception of and judgement about what has happened! So in the next chapter we will look more closely at the power of judgments and perception.

Chapter 10: I'll be the Judge of That!

"There is nothing either good or bad but thinking makes it so." William Shakespeare

Protagoras, an early Greek philosopher, put forward the following scenario to show that "man is the measure of all things".

If it were an average spring day in Athens, a man from a hot climate would conclude that it was a cold day, whilst a man from Sweden may refer to the day as warm. Protagoras' analogy simply demonstrates that there is no truth, only personal perspective and judgements that are purely subjective. Consequently, I will argue that they could be thought of as simply opinions. Every day we need to make judgements in order to operate in life. Making the right judgement at the right time can even be a matter of life or death. I need to make an instantaneous judgement about you the very first time that I meet you, for example —are you safe and friendly or are you a threat?

But most of the time we are making habitual judgements without questioning whether they are valid or not.

It is believed that everything that a child sees and hears between the ages of 0-7 is recorded and accepted unquestioningly, just as a tape recorder records everything faithfully. This is important because as babies and young children we learn everything from the trusted adults around us and because we depend on these adults for our survival we have to accept that they will teach us honestly. We trust that they will always act with our health and survival at heart. We do not as children possess the critical faculty to analyse, contest or compare their teachings in any meaningful way. These teachings form our fundamental, root beliefs and programs. These can potentially continue to run unquestioned throughout the rest of our lives unless at some point we consciously choose to question or remove them.

For example, I used to judge myself harshly if I felt I had spoken out of turn to someone in authority. I had been brought up to respect my elders and defer to anyone in authority and thus I spent most of my early adult life blindly accepting that this was appropriate behaviour. This programming made me feel as an adult 'guilty' at merely seeing a policeman, unable to question anyone in authority even if I clearly could see that something was wrong, and basically being put upon left, right and centre at work! I felt powerless and without a voice.

I never questioned this belief program and over time it became habitual and accepted even though it was detrimental to my life and experience. As a child, the belief program had worked for me, as following it meant avoiding confrontation and keeping out of trouble. In short it kept me in favour with adults. But as an adult, it left me feeling powerless and in some ways a victim or unworthy. I felt that because I was 'less' than that person in authority then my opinion didn't count and I didn't matter!

The good news is that once I became aware of the program, I made an informed judgment about whether it was still relevant and beneficial to me as an adult. As we saw in the LOA chapter, any negative emotion is a sign that you are not on track to what you want, or that you are not being the powerful person that your Higher Self knows you really are! As my beliefs developed about us all being equal and one, I could change my behaviour to be more assertive when I needed to be.

I can help you do this in your own lives through the work that the TOUR will guide you through. This work will help you to change that belief, remove it if you deem that it no longer serves you or adapt the positive aspects of it.

We can use the CORE to develop confidence and self-belief in order to say my opinion counts and I do not care what you think. I will stand up for myself on the occasions when it is right to do it and then I will feel excited about the future possibilities ahead.

The truth is that judgment is always personal to the person forming that judgment. Judgment is simply opinion! But as this is also true for us, we must accept that sometimes our judgement or opinion will be rejected. There is no-one alive that can be right all of the time and that includes you. If you wish to be heard, you must give that right to others too.

All events are neutral until we assign them meaning and I find this to be absolutely true in life. Let us look at the half glass full or glass half empty scenario. The state of the glass is whatever you judge it to be. It is one glass. If you judge it to be in one state, the other possible state arises too. Who would be right to say it is half full or vice versa? Often there is no right or wrong and sometimes there is just yes to both possibilities! It doesn't have to be this OR that. It can often be this AND that.

So who is qualified to be the judge and jury over our lives and who gave them that right? Who in reality has any right to judge anyone else? Judgement particularly in regards to another person is just opinion.

"The sun after all shines equally on all!" Matthew 5:43-48

I am advocating therefore that you become an independent thinker. I am advocating that you live your life and carry your own baggage and not everyone else's simply because you have not sorted out what is theirs as opposed to what is yours.

When was the last time that you looked at a belief program that you have and asked yourself where it came from and who it really serves? When did you last ask yourself if that belief program was actually true?

It is vital to realize that sometimes there are many beliefs and judgements at play in a situation and the problem is not what it first appears. I could falsely believe that the water leaking through an upstairs ceiling in my house is the problem. However, if the real problem stems from the tile missing from the roof of the house, unless I look past the ceiling leak I will never be able to reach the real root of the problem and thus be able to solve it permanently. Once you can discover your root beliefs, you will then need to make a judgement about what is the cost versus gain of dropping or keeping a particular program.

Let me give an example of this.

I had a client recently whose subconscious mind had been trying to bring to the light programming that was running about a fear of being alone.

This man was an only child and had been divorced for many years. He had a full social life and was financially independent, but he wanted to meet someone. He had a concern that he had been left 'on the shelf' and felt it was important to find someone to grow old with.

You may notice that this want already has fear (of growing old alone) attached to it! As you will come to see, this man's focus was not entirely on wanting a partner or at least wanting a partner for the right reasons.

When he initially came to me, I kept setting goals for him, small steps towards finding a partner. The man continuously made excuses as to why he had not taken these steps. I explained to him that as *he* was in control of his actions and decisions, there must be a stronger program running that was saying 'I *don't* want this to happen'. Eventually we discovered he had a huge tug of war going on around being independent versus wanting that special someone. Consequently, unbeknownst to him, there was a huge belief program that asserted 'you can't have it all'.

When I asked him where he had ever seen this belief written down, he simply insisted 'that everyone knows that'. We eventually discovered that this was a belief program from his parents and when I asked him for objective evidence that it was true, he could not give me any.

My client was also experiencing people around him having relationship issues which to him supported his argument that you couldn't have it all. He also reported that friends tended to ask him for help because they saw him as strong and capable. I explained to him that these two things were connected as they highlighted his negative fears about relationships and reinforced his positive belief in independence.

My client's main reason for wanting that 'special other' was to have someone to share the load with him in life so whilst he was independent, he also needed help. The two ends of the rope were pulling against each other - needing help versus being strong and independent and therefore do not need help! There was also a tug of war between 'relationships are trouble and I want a relationship'. The result was that he was stuck!

On the one hand, this man had been on his own so long that he prided himself on his self-resilience and ability to cope alone, but on the other he craved another person to care about him. But in order to admit another person into his life, he had to break down the wall of invincibility that he had built and allow himself to become vulnerable. If one doesn't have any barriers up there is nothing for anyone to push against. Then communication and the relationship itself can flow easily!

But the deepest obstacle to change for my client was the fact that he was actually fairly happy as he was. Although consciously he wanted to change one area of his life, the pull to do so was not as strong as it might have been because he knew subconsciously that he had a lot to lose by *getting* his wish. Therefore, the gain did not outweigh the potential costs. For him, the fear was that giving up his independence could actually be dangerous as evidenced by the troubled relationships around him. Through the lives of his friends, he was seeing his belief program that "you can't have it all!" manifested. It was almost as if he believed that because he was happy in some areas of his life at present, he was not allowed to have any more happiness!!

Craziness! But sadly many of us have that sort of belief system in place.

If you are keen to uncover your belief programs, the TOUR tools can be key in uncovering programs that not only counteract one another but that also prevent any possibility of moving forward!

The work for this gentleman then was to make a conscious judgement about what it was that he really wanted once he was aware of all the underlying issues. I always suggest using what I call the ABC strategy in this type of situation.

Designed to elicit change, the ABC strategy means taking the following steps:

An immediate Action (joining a dating site perhaps in the instance of my client).

A long term Behaviour to develop (such as allowing himself to be more vulnerable by asking for help when he needs it).

Choosing a new belief (setting affirmations that replace and overwrite old belief programs- E.g. I can and deserve to have it all).

We each have many differing levels of belief programs that affect our behaviour, but these can roughly be divided into three categories. These are:

1. Core beliefs—these are the accepted, unquestioned and deeply held beliefs that come from parents, educators, society, culture, history and the collective consciousness. These will colour the world that we believe that we live in.

2. Experiential beliefs—these are beliefs that we have picked up from personal life experiences and relationships. These will usually have some kind of personal emotional tie to them. They are likely to influence our judgments of who we are.

3. Background beliefs—these are beliefs based on things that we have heard, been told, seen in the media or on the TV. They are likely to be running as low level background programs. They may appear on the surface to be fairly innocuous and not directly related to us personally.

The category that it is most important to work on first is the experiential beliefs. This is because if there is an emotional tie present then you are likely to have layered either a stronger positive or negative judgement on it.

Labelling

In working on our experiential beliefs, it is important to remember that all emotions are experienced as sensations within the body. We judge and label them so that they give us guidance on pleasure or pain, power or powerlessness, alignment or misalignment with our greater soul.

Let us think about the case of this man from the perspective that everything is an opportunity to learn and evolve our greater self. On a deeper level his greater soul energy knew that he was already one with everything and everyone around him and thus he is never alone anyway. Lack of trust and faith in oneself is a judgement about who we think we are and how we view our place in the world. The negative emotion then was him being out of alignment with that knowledge and truth about who he really is!

As both anxiety and excitement usually occur in the tummy we could say that they are only sensations. The feeling of anxiety could be re-labelled as excitement, for example. By labelling the emotion differently; you are then able to start using it in a more positive manner.

To recognize negative emotion as feedback that you are on the wrong path allows you to deliberately choose a positive thought, belief or affirmation. This is your opportunity to pedal across the grass.

In the mindfulness work, we advise people just to sit and experience emotions simply as sensations until they dissipate away. If we can be conscious enough to catch ourselves at this choice point, we can remove all judgments and labels and decide how we want to see the reality before us.

Remember the event itself is always neutral.

You have the ability and power to choose every minute of every day. You are both the judge and the jury of your own life. You judge and then choose with your words, your thoughts, your emotions and actions the reality that you *will* experience.

We often reserve the harshest judgements for ourselves, but we must take care not to get into regret about our past actions.

The past is past. The only truly healthy action is to accept that whatever labels we gave to an emotion or an event was right at that time and in those circumstances.

Self Esteem

Often our judgement about ourselves allows other people an opportunity to treat us accordingly. After all, people can only treat us as we allow them to. People can only affect us if we allow them to and again this really is a measure of our own self esteem.

In psychology, self-esteem is a term used to describe a person's overall appraisal of his or her own worth. Your evaluation of your self-esteem is made up of belief programs about yourself. Some of these beliefs will have come from your observation and acceptance of other people's reflection and judgements about you. Even self-esteem is in some ways just your opinion about whom you think you are and it will either limit or propel you forward in life accordingly.

We are brought up with a whole raft of rules and dictates reinforced by religious, historical, social and family codes that may or may not be in our best interests to follow. These are the aforementioned core beliefs that seem unchangeable and unchallengeable. Which of these beliefs you choose to follow, or not follow, is nothing to do with me; it is all your choice.

I do suggest, however, that instead of following these beliefs blindly you start to seriously question where they have come from, who they serve and whether you even need them. Many of our rules are pushed towards us for the benefit of others and not necessarily for the benefit of the individual. They are really about social control, fairness and cohesiveness. On occasion they are just there to elicit behaviour that makes other people happy.

Think about the rules your parents enforced and encouraged, for example. Imagine as a child that you were constantly told 'speak when you are spoken to', for instance. This is a rule that says to the child you are inferior; your opinion does not count.

If you received this edict as a child, you may develop good manners but you would need to question as an adult whether it still served you. Is this a program that now means you are meek and unable to stand up for yourself? Does it mean that you allow yourself to be bullied at work or downtrodden in other areas of your life? Is this relevant for you today as an adult?

Of course, this program may have a positive twist – such as doing well in your career because you are an excellent and obedient worker.

Once you start this work, it tends to lead to a questioning of everything so you can clear out the old programs and make way for more useful new ones. In some ways this work is akin to de-fragmenting the computer of your mind. Just as your home computer collects more and more programs, we as humans do as well. You do not have to wait until you are trading in your body for a new one to start with a clear and de-fragmented processor. We can start now to clear the old programs, remove the back ground viruses and upgrade to the latest and more suitable software to do the job in hand. When you start to look at the beliefs and programs running today, it is also worth remembering that many of our rules and laws were set in a different time frame and may no longer be relevant today.

Another concept that may affect your self-esteem is the feeling of power that you hold over your own life. The American psychologist Julian Rotter called this the locus of control.

The locus of control deals with how much control a person has over the different events in their lives and how this affects their happiness and self-esteem.

Generally a person deemed to have an internal locus of control will feel that they have a high level of control over their lives while those with an external locus will feel powerless and believe that outside forces are to blame for events.

Thankfully as adults we can; become free thinkers, to speak freely and if we so choose to make a difference in the world. Therefore there is no logical reason why we all should not have internal loci of control. The main reason some do not is because they may be ignorant of the fact that they are powerful creators of their reality.

Sometimes, people become unsettled when I suggest that society's rules and dictates need not be followed unfailingly and I am certainly in no way advocating crime. Ask yourself this, however - do you not steal, cheat or kill because the law says that you should not or because you judge it as wrong for you personally and thus choose not to? Or could it be perhaps because you have no true sense of lack?

People that end up in jails are generally people that feel powerless, bored, angry, hurt and unloved. I refuse to believe that any baby is born evil. We are all the product of our conditioning. When all of our emotional needs are met and we have our basic material needs met, there is no need for us to hurt others or take anything from them.

The Buddhists have a truly wonderful description of 'ignorance'. For them, the word is not used in the same way as it is by most languages or cultures. Ignorance, according to the Buddhists, refers to a lack of knowledge and by implication understanding. This really means that a person who is ignorant has merely not been taught better or been shown a better way. Their reasoning is then that we should feel and show them compassion and forgiveness because:

1. There but for the grace of God go us all. If you are not in that situation or experiencing any of those lacks that I have listed above to a serious degree, you are blessed and have been fortunate enough to have been born into a good environment. You may also have had the benefit of good teachers and role models.

2. At some point in our lives, if we do not remain consciously aware of how we are creating our lives we too may fall into a place of lack.

3. We cannot cherry pick which parts of creation we choose to own. You are the one in the mirror ball and thus those negative

qualities that you are seeing in others are actually in you too- perhaps to a lesser degree.

We all have lied, cheated and stolen. Yes, even you. We lie about our age or do not tell the truth exactly. A lie is a lie even if you appease yourself by calling it white. By doing something in our own personal interest at work then you are guilty of stealing the company's time. To own something negative, it doesn't have to be the exact same depth, strength or type of event. It is the essence of that quality that you have to recognize as yours.

Accept that anyone struggling that comes into your awareness is a reflection of you or accept them as your greatest teacher because they also show us contrast. They reflect that which we do not own or want for ourselves. From that gift which we can see more clearly that which we do want. Therefore, it is essential to refrain from making arbitrary judgements about other people especially from a place of stereotypes or old patterns. Everyone is a part of you, is as good as you, struggles as you do and deserves your compassion and tolerance.

Judgements can divide us unnecessarily.

In conclusion then it is crucial that every individual accepts full responsibility for their life which is created and determined by their personal choices and conscious efforts. This ensures an internal locus of control.

At the end of the day you are only the sum of your judgements about yourself!

The change from a victim mentality towards empowering ownership brings with it immense rewards. The ability to change is natural to us all. The natural movement towards growth and evolution is the 'factory setting' that we are all born with. And change is easy!

Your mind is a beautiful garden and these judgements etc are like the weeds that can take over if you do not keep up with the gardening. However, if you do not pull up the root, the garden will look lovely for a while but then the weeds will keep reappearing

Chapter 11: Beliefs and Programs

"It is better to conquer yourself than to win a thousand battles. Then the victory is yours." Buddha

Before we go any further, I would like to remind you of my strawberry-moment story earlier in the book. It is important to remember and to keep reinforcing to yourself, particularly if you are very new to any of these concepts, that no-one holds 'the bag' of truth. You can choose whatever truth serves you best. This is an environment where you are creating by the nature of your belief, *everything* that is occurring 'out there'- without exception. You are creating the truth for you.

When I trained as a hypnotherapist, I was taught about the power of suggestion and repetition. That is why throughout the text you will find me reiterating and reinforcing the same basic concepts. The more you read them, the more you are pedalling across the grass and making new ruts in the brain.

A belief is a thought that you practiced well and these beliefs are collected from a mixture of information and values given to us from others and from society or culture. We also collect beliefs from our past experiences.

Alongside our beliefs, a range of pre-suppositions exist which are values that are taken for granted or accepted without proof. I would say that the two most common but damaging suppositions is that change, especially changing who you are, is difficult and that you are powerless to change your life and circumstances. These are beliefs or suppositions that you may have taken on board, but never really questioned. These are limiting beliefs because they severely restrict your personal potential.

I believe that you are *not* powerless and that change is *not* difficult once you are aware of why you hold a particular belief.

'I am powerful and change is easy' I suggest you make this your new mantra right away!

Limiting beliefs often run continuously and form part of the self-perpetuating feedback loop which does exactly what it says on the tin. You run the program: change is difficult (this is the belief). You see the result: I cannot quit smoking, for example (this is the feedback that you are seeing) and thus the program is reinforced: See, I told you change is difficult (self-perpetuating).

Believing is seeing! 'Change is difficult' becomes just that because believing is seeing and not the other way around. This is an important difference because one says that you are in control (if you are conscious and aware of your belief programs) while the other says that you are a victim to events.

If you accept that you are creating your reality then it must be logical that you are creating it from your beliefs because it is your reality mirror. Everything is being generated by your personal belief programming. That's why the car manufacturer Henry Ford's "If you think you can or you think you can't either way you will be right" quote is so apt here. You get exactly what you believe you will get consciously or subconsciously. If you think you can or you think you can't then either way you will create that in your reality. It is important to remember here that the subconscious mind always has your health, wellbeing and safety as its central purpose. It will doggedly create your reality from the strongest belief or do its utmost to protect you from your strongest fears. It is a loyal servant.

However, what that actually looks like and what you experience in reality may not be what *you* (as the conscious being that experiences the outcomes) may immediately feel is in your best interests. It may on the surface not appear to be a positive event or circumstance! But do not allow there to be any self-recrimination for anything you have created so far.

Responsibility Not Blame

This work requires that you take total responsibility for all of your creations without exception even for those things that may not have gone well or that we regret or feel guilty about. Please understand that there is no blame. Blame, I believe, is accusatory and has a negative vibration whereas responsibility is more empowering.

In considering blame, first of all, you must answer an obvious question: how can you blame yourself for something that you created in the past when you did not understand the rules of the game?

Let us use a game of billiards as an example.

What if you were to pick up and move a ball with your hand whilst playing and consequently you were accused of cheating? If the rules had never been explained to you, how could you know that your action was cheating? We could say that the action of picking up the ball was not cheating but ignorance as you had not been taught well the rules of the game and so were unaware of a vital piece of information.

How could you make sense of or survive in a world that did not follow strict rules? All games have to have rules to allow the structure, flow and end point of the game. It is the rules themselves that make the game playable.

If you continued to move the billiard ball after you were made aware of the rules then that would be cheating but more importantly it would be a choice. How and what you create is a choice- albeit an extremely empowering or potentially damaging one because every choice brings up a consequence. Cause and effect if you like.

Often it is when we do not want one particular consequence of a choice that we say we have no choice. But that is not true. In a world of free will there is always choice. When we look more closely into the area of language and its effects on our lives and programming, that nuance of truth will be extremely significant. 'I always have a choice' is a belief that makes you powerful whereas 'I have no choice' will make you a victim to life and circumstances every time.

Often when I am coaching clients, I ask a question about why that person is doing a particular action, behaving in a certain way or has a particular belief and they will say, 'I don't know'. I will immediately reply 'you do know. You are the only one that knows because you are choosing to do it!' I am very strict about not allowing them to continue to believe that they are puppets to their minds because that is a very disempowering way to live. I will never allow anyone to play victim in life!

The problem is that we are usually really good at rationalising, justifying and making any excuse for our behaviour particularly if we do not know consciously why we are doing it. So we make up stories to make sense of our world. The biggest fictitious story by the way is that a habit is beyond our control!

If the process of projection, for example, is not understood it can appear as though things are happening to you. We rationalise things through nebulous concepts such as luck or 'fate' without ever really questioning or drilling down into what fate or luck really are. What is luck? Good fortune you may say? When everything works out for your benefit perhaps? Well, if you understand that you are actually saying that you created and were given exactly what you asked for, is that not the same thing? Saying 'I am not a lucky person' may just be rationalisation and justification for a subconscious or un-owned belief program that 'nothing ever goes well for me.'

If I gently encourage clients to look for the gain of a choice, it usually becomes clear very quickly that there are other programs or beliefs running in their subconscious minds. A good example would be smokers who repeatedly try and fail to quit. They know logically and rationally why they want to stop smoking, but they still believe that they cannot give up because it is a habit.

But what is a habit other than a behaviour that has been repeated so often that it has become an unquestioned automatic pattern?

A habit is simply something that you do repeatedly and often without thinking. It has no mysterious power other than it has now become unquestioned. At the end of the day, it is just another program running. But beneath the program probably lies a belief that habits are difficult to break. Once again that is a limiting belief and absolutely not true. It is, however, our 'get out clause' or permission slip to be able to continue the behaviour.

One of the most difficult beliefs to overcome simply because it is so ingrained and unquestioned is again, that change is difficult. But this is just a program!

When I ask smokers who is in control of their arms and hands, they will always tell me that they are. Then who, I ask, puts the cigarette into their mouths? Now they start to see that it is a choice at least on some level. Often they have bought into a program that says smoking is addictive but that is only a belief. I am not saying that stopping smoking may not take time or may not be uncomfortable, but it is the collective consciousness (core) belief that a habit is hard to break that is the real problem. The fact that this truth is reinforced constantly by everyone around us is not because it is true but because we all have the program running!

If it was absolutely an unbreakable law of the universe, then why is it that some people can quit for good and do so in the blink of an eye? Most of us can think of someone who managed to give up smoking immediately once their mind was focused or the doctor informed them that if they didn't stop smoking they would be dead within months. The only difference that allows them to suddenly find this power is that the risk of continuation of said behaviour no longer outweighs the gain at that point.

That person now chooses the strongest belief of gain which is to live!

Please read that sentence again because it is the simplest way that I can reinforce to you how you are choosing to create your reality. Every choice is yours. In every behaviour —even seemingly negative behaviours —there must be a gain that is stronger than the opposite action.

The question to ask is: Why would I choose something that I say I do not want? What is the gain of that choice? There will always without fail be a gain!

Habits do not suddenly become easy to break. Instead, the beliefs of the individual have changed. The believing immediately became the seeing!

Wake up to the fact that not only are you being influenced by the cultural and majority beliefs of everyone around you but that you are influenced on many other levels too. Habits and addictions are reinforced continuously by advertisers, for example, because there are billions of pounds to be made by people failing to lose weight, stop smoking or stay healthy! If you do not believe me, spend a few hours thinking about TV adverts.

Look beneath the superficial messages. Note how many are selling you products that reinforce your inability to do something for yourself or ask you to buy into their particular form of help.

We do not question enough the information that affects us. Sadly it is easier to blame our behaviour on a habit because we are ignorant or have become somewhat lazy or reluctant to accept full responsibility for the creation of everything in our lives!

Your subconscious mind is continuously projecting out into the world simply to show you in the mirror that actually you are a powerful being and that you can give up easily. You could spend all day looking for evidence on the internet of all the people who have given up smoking 'just like that'. Once your focus is on success, your vibration will change to one of hope and excitement and your neuro-net of positive outcomes and beliefs will grow into a strong positive pathway of choice and then success will be much more likely.

If you do the TOUR work and remove all the associated programming in your mind, I dare say that success could come much quicker too!

With the arising of the thought 'I cannot' there is the potential for 'I can' because everything in life is duality, remember? And again whether you believe you can or you believe you cannot, it is your belief that will determine the outcome.

It is pure mechanics to change the brain programming. One only needs to use the same process of repetition that built the pathway in the first place. A belief is simply a thought that you have practiced well. No more and no less. Change is easy.

It is now a belief because it has become a repeated, well-practised thought. It has become so comfortable and unquestioned to the point that it feels true. If you remember back to my analogy of taking the same path every day until there is a rut in the ground, you can see that it is the continual repetition that strengthens the neuro-net in the brain: smoking, addictive, hard to break, relaxing, enjoyable, my only vice and so on.

If I change the belief program into the affirmation 'I am in control of my actions', I must also allow time for the new belief to become the new program running via the process of repetition. Notice that I have not said 'I am a non-smoker.' This is firstly because an affirmation must be powerful and in the present tense. Secondly, the universe is responding to the subject of the affirmation. What is the subject of 'I am a non-smoker'? It is smoking! Thus to go a more general phrasing also ensures that you are then not bringing up any associated programs that may be surreptitiously linked to smoking. Maybe the fact that the first time you smoked you won approval from a guy or a girl you fancied is still playing out in the back of the mind and so you may connect together smoking and being attractive. 'I am in control of my actions' will also help many other areas of your life as well!

Immediately the client may start to say, 'but that's not true, I don't believe it'. So I add 'yet'!

Yet says it is only a matter of time and I am on my way. The addition of the word 'yet' changes the vibration from one of being stuck into one of hope and moving forward.

A really good technique in changing habits is to have a band on your wrist and to change it to the other wrist each time you catch yourself saying or thinking something negative or detrimental. As you change the band and break the train of thought you can then replace it with the new positive affirmation, repeating it constantly with feeling.

This focuses your mind really quickly on how your thoughts are running generally, but also makes you aware of your thought and speech patterns. From the LOA point of view, it also reaffirms your focus on what you do want and builds the new pathway in the brain!

The only way to build new and different pathways in the brain is to keep cycling over the grass. That is to keep practising the new affirmation repeatedly until it starts to feel like the truth.

Whilst you are not using the cycle path of negative thinking that rut gradually disappears on its own until only the new rut of positive thinking is left. As you have repeated this new mantra so many times, it will become the automatic pathway of choice. 'I am in control of my actions' will then feel like and become the absolute truth for you and you will see evidence to reinforce that.

At that point, the mind will start filtering for evidence to confirm that 'I am now in control of my actions' and will search for confirmation of that around us in our lives. The new belief becomes your new reality. To make sense of the transition period however, you will start to see that you are craving a cigarette less or that you may suddenly discover that you can go a whole day without even thinking of it. Sometimes, the signpost will not say Glasgow but the A1 remember. The sign of change in this scenario may be as random keeping your cool when the neighbours' children break your window with their football because now you think, 'I am in control of my actions'.

For the smoking client, the belief that s/he is addicted and powerless to stop is simply the belief or program that is currently showing itself to be the strongest, most engrained or most important program at that time.

The next part of the programming is to look at the gains of keeping this habit. If there were simply no gain, the individual would be able to kick the habit by themselves. So whatever gains the client gets from a habit; such as stress release in the case of smoking, these will support the main belief program.

You have to accept that underneath every behaviour is a positive intention or a sub/conscious gain, otherwise you would not choose to continue behaving that way. Sometimes, we choose negatively or by default because we do not want to accept the consequences of the alternative option. We then believe that we have *no choice* but in truth you always have a choice.

Let us imagine I have a job that I absolutely hate but I feel I have no choice except to keep it because of the recession or my age or my pension or whatever other reason. Consequently, I feel stuck, powerless and essentially a victim. But if I accept that I do have a choice then I can at least go into work and feel empowered and in control of my life. Or I can choose not to go in and accept the consequences of homelessness or a difficult and frugal retirement. That is a fact. No one can drag me into work by my hair. There is always choice - fact.

By telling myself that there are wonderful gains by having this job then I become empowered. If I am able to focus my attention on the fact that I am luckier than the two million people who are unemployed or keep my attention on something that I do like about the job then I can feel happier. If I say thank you every moment I feel negatively about the job because I recognise it pays my rent and bills then I am more likely to enjoy the work in any case.

This would be effective even though nothing 'out there' has changed. As everything in this vibrational universe is thought based, changing your mind changes your vibration and gradually changes your reality mirror because it is being created from within. It is also hugely affected by your vibrational state because it is affected by your attitude to that experience.

Believing Is Seeing

The complexities and layering of how the mind operates are incredible. However, once you start to understand its codes and rules then you can start to use those same rules to program it differently.

You can only become a successful player of billiards, for example, if you understand the rules and practise a lot.

Since it is YOU that is filtering incoming data and projecting out information from the place where that very belief is located then of course it is logical that you are going to see evidence that supports that belief. Again, believing is seeing.

It is important to reiterate here that the brain is matching patterns and creating what it believes or expects to be 'out there' from incoming data from the senses. As we have discovered your reality is in some ways a perceptual construction based on your existing beliefs about it.

It is also crucial to understand that whatever you perceive with regard to your feelings about yourself and your life creates a chemical and emotional response in the body. Any perception of an event is your *subjective truth* once sieved through the filters of your existing thoughts, feelings and beliefs about yourself. Whatever you perceive as occurring 'out there' stimulates a reaction from within you and this in turn reinforces your perception. We may even call it a self-fulfilling prophecy.

Let us say, for example, that our friend Robert has been feeling insecure and nervous about lunching with some important business colleagues. At the lunch, his hand is shaking and he knocks a glass of wine over. He is now in such a heightened state of anxiety that he proceeds to drop his knife or say the wrong thing and descends into a pit of self-loathing. He continues to beat himself up for days afterwards despite no real damage occurring.

But sadly for Robert he has now reinforced his deeply held belief program that he is clumsy and stupid. This belief is probably something that was trained into his brain in childhood. Most of us in that situation would apologise, make a joke, mop up the wine and then never give it another thought. But for Robert, the incident launches a series of associated beliefs that are further reinforced by his emotional feeling. In other words, it is a self-perpetuating feedback loop.

A single emotion causes the release of a peptide (the key) which then searches for the matching 'lock' in a cell. A chemical reaction in the cell then ensues, that matches and perpetuates the original emotional state. By experiencing the same emotions every day, the same peptides create the same habitual reactions and feelings every day. Robert would have many 'locks' for clumsiness for which his brain will search out opportunities to create 'keys' for. That is why to Robert his clumsiness feels out of his control and is in fact something that he just is.

This has become his habitual perception of his self and his world! But again, all events are essentially neutral until we judge them. The only truth here is that a glass has been knocked over. Everything else is simply Robert's story about it.

If we can accept that all circumstances are neutral and we are the ones that project meaning onto situations, how and why do we select the same patterns?

Let us now ask ourselves:

How do you perceive yourself and your world?

Is this a true perception?

Is there current evidence or is this merely an ingrained belief about yourself from the past?

Where and from whom did these perceptions originate and why?

Whose voice/what tapes are playing in your mind?

What stories do you tell yourself about your role and abilities in life?

Is it an up to date story?

What evidence are you using to support that story about who and what you are?

Are you happy with those stories?

In my life, for many years unbeknown to me, my mother's voice played in my mind, saying "there's never enough money". I can still vividly remember her saying we can't afford this or that.

But the reality of my childhood was that we always had everything we needed or wanted. We always had presents on birthdays and Christmas, holidays, food on the table etc.

My mother would say that was because they always put the children first but that her and my father still struggled. I have no doubt that this is true, but my point is that the mantra of "there's never enough money" was her reality and not mine. My reality was that there was always enough.

When as an adult, I became aware of that program that had been running unquestioned since childhood; I was quite shocked to see how I had been living through my mother's perspective. If I looked honestly at my adult life, I too believed; "There is never enough". I lived frugally, saved what I could and certainly felt very poor indeed. So in some ways we could say that was my perceived truth. However, it was not a fact.

When I really looked at my years as an independent adult, I was shocked to find that actually there always was enough money – but only just enough.

My mother's program was so ingrained that I lived as if I was poor when the reality was that all my bills were paid, I had little debt and plenty of holidays. When I realised the huge gap between my perceived and actual reality, I immediately started to change that programming. Interestingly, for the next few years I actually had less income but felt a whole lot richer. This again was a huge lesson for me about whose life I was living!

'There is never enough' is obviously a fear-based belief that will elicit deep feelings of insecurity. This program of poverty consciousness was extremely limiting because as I felt so poor and insecure about money, it prevented me doing things, buying things or moving forward in a positive way. Essentially, I was living in constant fear of poverty and lack. No wonder I was miserable and depressed all the time! My beliefs had created what I was seeing in my life.

The scariest part is that LOA worked perfectly even though I knew nothing about it at the time. As my focus and certainly my vibration were on managing my resources, I always stayed in the place of having to manage my resources!

Just as an interesting aside about affirmations, when I created an affirmation to change this I would proudly recite "there is always enough". Good old LOA duly ensured that indeed there was always just enough. It was only when I really started to understand LOA that I realised that I needed to start focusing on living in abundance if that was what I wanted. I duly changed that affirmation to 'I am abundant, wealthy and healthy' and so I am. The language and subject of your affirmation needs to be thought about very, very carefully!!!

In truth that excellent metaphor about how we can choose to view our glass as half full or half empty is also relevant here. I believed that I was poor and in constant need when I could have chosen to see that actually I always had more than enough.

If we can determine abundance as always having the means to do, be or have whatever we need in a particular moment then I have always been abundant. In effect, I was abundant but perceived myself to be poor and saw my glass as half empty. Everything is perception!

Affirmations
Once you have decided that you have a program running that you wish to overwrite, the way to do it is via affirmations.

I want to reinforce this point that affirmations are not airy-fairy rote phrases about wishful thinking. The repetition of an affirmation is a powerful way to reprogram the mind, to create a new pathway across the grass.

The repetition of the affirmation is the pedalling that takes you forward on the new journey.

But affirmations are more complex than you may first think and this is why sometimes it may appear that they do not work. A crucial factor in the success of an affirmation is that it must be done with feeling.

Try saying this three times:

'I can succeed'

Now sit and think about all the many times that you have succeeded: look for any evidence no matter how small or trivial that you are already a success. This will start to fire up and connect the neuro-nets that already exist in the brain for success.

Now repeat the phrase again three times with even more feeling and with the genuine realization of how successful you already are.

"I can succeed".....celebrate it, jump for joy in your heart and be grateful that you already are a success!

This is the vibration that you need to have to create the feeling that you are already a success. If you do not feel the state that you are trying to affirm, it will be very difficult to get there. Your words will just be empty and meaningless. This is also the reason that affirmations must be stated in positive language and in the present tense because to act as if the desire has already been granted is a powerful message to the brain. You have to be the vibration of wealth before it appears.

As Mahatma Gandhi said, "You must be the change that you wish to see in the world." Gandhi's statement speaks to us about action - if you want the world to change then you have to move to do it - but it also speaks to us about *being* our truth. Being happy first allows you to actually attract things that make you feel happy. Your world changes because it is the believing that creates the seeing.

I believe that as soon as you make a statement of intent to change, then the universe delivers. A faithful servant, it will obediently and immediately give you an opportunity to practice and demonstrate your success. However, most of us fail to realise that the universe is actually trying to help us when it provides an opportunity that includes the negative behaviour we are trying to break. Often we give up on our intention and decide that we have chosen the wrong time to change this behaviour.

For example, on New Year's Eve you may resolve to give up smoking. Let us assume that you smoke to ease stress and because it calms you down. On New Year's Day you will find that there immediately appears a stressful situation, but because you have not prepared yourself for an opportunity so soon after making your resolution, you say "I need a cigarette. I have chosen the wrong day to give up smoking".

Pause for a moment and ask yourself:

If that stressful situation had not appeared, how could you really know that you had given up smoking for stress? The universe is simply giving you an opportunity to practice your desire and to know that you can be strong and decline to smoke. This is the only way to know that you have given up smoking for good. It is presenting you with the chance to succeed!

Everything in your reality is about you and everything is created as a servant to your cause.

So whenever you make a strong statement of intent, remember that the universe will provide you with the opportunity to apply that intent. Moreover, the knowledge of this allows you to prepare your strategy. As the American military say, "Fail to prepare and prepare to fail".

Language

Just as we can see our thoughts and beliefs by looking into the reality mirror, we can also hear them by listening to what we say to others, particularly the language that we use and the stories that we tell ourselves.

Students in my classes quickly become very sensitive to how they speak because I make it a priority to draw their attention to the stories that they are telling themselves.

In fact it quickly becomes a standing joke at how people cringe when they say inadvertently, the forbidden words!

If a student says repeatedly 'I can't meditate' or 'I can't stop the thoughts' then that is exactly what he or she will create in his/her mind as a belief program and it will then become reality.

I will usually start by bringing the student's awareness to what they are declaring and add 'yet' to the end of their limiting beliefs.

Let us pause and feel the difference between stating:

'I cannot stop my thoughts...'

And:

'I cannot stop my thoughts yet...'

Doesn't that second statement feel different? Those three little letters say a huge amount to your mind. They say there is hope. 'Yet' infers that you can do this with practise.

Remember that everything in your reality is created by the stories that you tell yourself, your beliefs and your vibration. The vibrational difference between these two statements will manifest very different outcomes in your reality. What you think and feel about any subject is what you will get. It is pure physics. It is the Law of Attraction.

The other thing that I will not allow in my class is the word TRY. Try has failure written all over it. It says there is a high possibility that you will fail before you have even started whatever it is that you are attempting to achieve.

Again let us pause and feel the difference between declaring;

'I will try to stop my thoughts'

And

'I will stop my thoughts'

The vibration is again extremely different between the two. I will try has a current running underneath it of 'I do not expect to succeed, success is beyond me, I am not really focussed and dedicated to achieving this, I don't really care about the outcome.' A real sense of *knowing* is missing.

If those are your real thoughts about the subject then that is fine, but at least be honest about what you are really saying. Otherwise, if you do not achieve that thing that you are declaring to the world that you want to achieve, when you fail it will just reinforce any existing negative programming that you have. It then appears to become a self-fulfilling prophecy when really it may just have been lack of commitment, lack of desire and honesty in the first place!

In some ways, you can imagine how difficult it is to be able to monitor everything that you say. But if you just start to practice telling the truth (at least to yourself) and being clear about what that truth is you will be well on your way. It is also a wonderful practice to listen to what other people say about themselves because it makes you more aware of how we all use language.

I often hear someone use a phrase and realise I say that or I think that too. In some ways that is no surprise as they are all aspects of me in the mirror anyway, but on another level it is an excellent way to notice belief programs running that you may not be conscious of.

I recently was listening to a friend talking about how much food and drink was good or bad for you and she made the statement about "everything in moderation".

I heard myself agree with that. Then it hit me like a thunderbolt. If that was a belief or a program about life that I already knew and recognized, it would *have* to be having an effect somewhere on my life.

When I looked around, I discovered that that was a huge program running. I live totally experiencing everything in moderation!

I laughed out loud for many reasons. Firstly, I love the way when doing this work every minute of every day, there is always a lesson or some uncovering to be learnt. Secondly, I realised that I could still have such a huge limiting program running without being aware of it on any level. On closer inspection, I realised this was another layer of associative thinking related to my income. I had successfully changed the 'there is never enough' program years ago, but was now being limited by this belief because in my many areas of my life I certainly acted or experienced things in moderation!

Self-awareness work is often compared to peeling the layers of an onion. You may successfully peel away one layer at a time, but at some point you will reach the root program that when released will free you forever on that subject.

It is then incredibly enlightening to listen to what declarations you make about who you really are. 'I am' is said to be the most powerful statement in the Universe. I am is a statement that says it has already happened or that you are 'acting as if' the gift has already been given, acting as if this is already your truth.

So when you declare, for example, 'I am in control of my actions' this is a clear and definite statement made to the universe, even if it may not be strictly true in that very moment. If that vibration is achieved with a strong intent that is totally focused AND as long as there are no other programs running subconsciously that go against that intent AND there are no hidden gains to the contrary, then that statement *must* become a manifestation into your reality.

Whilst we are on the subject of language, the other word to look out for is 'should'. Should implies a vibration of resistance from the outset otherwise you would be saying want to, can or will. 'Should' contains an air of victimhood to the demands of life, within it. The work is about looking at what you really would prefer, honestly, in the scenario in which you are using the word. Otherwise resentment is sure to follow!

'I should' usually has a 'but' in the following sequence of words, which leads you to the underlying contradiction in feelings of wanted and unwanted. 'Should' exposes the quality of the duality of wanted and unwanted; the tug of war between the two ends of the rope. There are definitely times when 'should' can be the most positive option, but one must be honest and conscious about that choice. Change the language to 'I am going to' or 'I want to' because that is more truthful and definitely more empowering than should!

The Subconscious Mind

In the game of life, the fundamental rule is that your strongest belief is the one that you will manifest into your reality. It is *your* responsibility to ensure that it is a *conscious* choice about which belief manifests in every situation.

Because there is simply too much information in our environment to take in, we use beliefs and judgement filters to ensure that only the most personally salient information hits our conscious awareness.

However, the subconscious mind is obviously still recording faithfully, without judgement - and I propose storing - absolutely everything else.

It is now believed that there is never a time in which the subconscious mind is not active even in deep sleep or under anaesthesia. In deep trance state, things that doctors have said during anaesthesia have been successfully 'remembered' by the patient, which shows that the mind never closes down completely. Even when a person is thought to be in deep coma or a persistent vegetative state (PVS), he or she may still possess limited 'consciousness'.

When placed under an MRI scanner, a test showed that the brains of some people diagnosed with PVS still lit up if their names were called.

As adults, and especially these days because of the availability of 24/7 information, it is vital that we are conscious and choosy about what things we allow ourselves to be exposed to.

However, we must also be aware that it is also likely that you may have subconscious belief programs that have a strong emotional tie and / or an initial sensitizing event affecting you every day. As you will see in the next chapter, sometimes something happened in your early life that had a serious emotional effect on you, and which continues to play out as a set of beliefs and associated programs of behaviour in your present life.

For example, I had a client who nearly drowned when she was around seven but who had no conscious memory of it. It was only when she tried to learn to swim as an adult that she found a problem because she could not let go of the float. Strangely enough, when she did let go of the float with her right arm, it would be as if she was being pulled under by it. The natural reaction would be simply to put your feet down. Once we had brought the forgotten memory to the surface and dealt with it, we then had to deal with releasing the muscle memory so that if she let go of the float today she would stay horizontal. The release of the muscle memory resulted in the resurfacing of many other repressed emotions.

I have developed the TOUR guides to help you decipher the belief system in the mind, but also to be able to change or remove the programs. That is why it is important to complete the work with the meditation TOUR. It is vital not only to complete the ABC of change, but also to clear the old programming on the physical energy, body and spiritual level for this very reason.

Many of our beliefs and programs cause a physical reaction and the most potentially debilitating of those are fears. But as you will come to see, fear programs are actually just another opportunity to be more, to grow, to evolve and to take your power back! We'll look at this more in the next chapter.

Chapter 12: Fears

"God does not call the qualified. God qualifies the called"
Exodus 3:2-14

I believe that the facing of fear is actually less frightening and much less disabling than living with the underlying feeling of helplessness that unexplored fears and phobias engender.

Fears play a huge part in all our lives, but it is usually a very negative part. A sense of fear is, however, an innate and necessary aspect of our biological make-up. It is a key factor in our ability to stay safe and alive.

It is important to recognise that fear is a natural and normal aspect of everyday lives and that we will never be totally free of things that cause us fear. Acceptance of this fact can be incredibly freeing.

If you can accept this as reality and know that the only way to be free is to face it head on, it can allow you to avoid years of potential suffering. In this work with the TOUR, I aim to show you that a fear is merely another belief program of the mind. It is not you and so it can be removed from the computer.

The sad truth is that in these days and times, many of the things that we are fearful of are not real survival issues in and of themselves. Unfortunately though, these fears can still have an incredibly limiting effect on our ability to live a meaningful or exciting life.

Any fear will set off the fight, flight or freeze (FFF) response mechanism in the body to some degree.

The FFF system operates in this way. If you sense danger, the body either prepares to fight to defend itself, freeze and hope not to be seen, or finally to flee and run away. These were the only options primitive man had. As the system was originally designed purely as a survival strategy, the body prioritizes sending blood, oxygen and energy to the limbs and away from the brain as logic or planning are not necessary at that point. I believe the FFF system—although this may be an over simplification—has an off/on switch. There is either fear or there is no fear although there are obviously different degrees of fear. In this way, I find it easier to deal with fear at the basic level at which we need to understand it here.

If you think about it logically, if you are constantly sending the majority of blood, oxygen and energy to the limbs, what would be left to replenish and repair any of your major organs or to boost the immune or the digestive system? Just as your car will start to break down if you drive it continuously without replenishing it with oil so the physical body will break down if in the long term it doesn't receive the things it needs.

I believe though that a lot of illnesses, particularly stressed-based ones such as Irritable Bowel Syndrome, may have something to do with our living in a constant state of fight or flight. I guess this would be analogous to having the switch stuck on the 'on' position without our conscious awareness of it.

We have become so frightened of life in some ways and so obsessed with health and safety that our lives have become completely overtaken by fear. We need to start looking at acceptable levels of fear and risk as this will enable us to free ourselves a little.

Your body, for example, has an amazingly complex and intelligently designed immune system that if not hindered by us is more than capable of protecting us from a few household germs. Yet we as a society seem obsessed with 100% annihilation of all germs. How will your immune system learn to deal with and develop strategies to fight germs if you never expose yourself to them? Remember, use it or lose it!

Fear of Loss and Pain
So let us turn our attention to dealing with fear in a more healthy way by exploring what it really is.

I think of fears as falling broadly into two main categories: fears of loss and fear of emotional pain. At their core then fears appear to be avoidance programs; the two fears are basically avoidance of suffering loss or of experiencing pain. One could argue that the two could actually just be one program of avoidance since any loss causes pain by its very nature. Even the ultimate fear of death is actually loss of life.

Limiting our growth and achievements, these programs can run consciously or subconsciously within us and can also be disguised as a fear of something completely different.

One of the biggest and most disguised fears is fear of death. People say that they are afraid of flying, heights or germs when really if ever played out to its full potential, it becomes apparent that their true fear is fear of death (loss of life). One of the biggest things that helped to free me from the fear of death was courageously facing death head on.

'Face the fear and walk straight through it' as the Zen Buddhists propose.

As a hypnotherapist, I have learnt about this subject first hand as I have performed more and more past life regressions. I studied and underwent my own life between lives regression. In deep regression, you can access not only your past life story, but also what happens in between incarnations, i.e. step into the 'spirit world' as such. For me, to have this experience was incredibly life changing and it allowed me to release any fear of death.

Once you find some way to convince yourself that you *will* continue on in some form after 'death' then you can really start to live.

If you are interested in this topic, there is so much excellent research collating Near Death Experiences such as that done by Pim Van Lommel MD in his wonderful book "Consciousness Beyond Life" and the work of the Canadian biochemist and professor of psychiatry Ian Pretyman Stevenson. Stevenson studied over 40 cases of children that have knowledge of their previous lives, gathering physical evidence relating to the often unusual birthmarks and birth defects of said children. He claimed that he had often been able to match wounds recorded in post-mortem records for the past-life individual that the children described.

As I discovered, science also supports an after-life of sorts. Physicists say that I am energy and energy can never be destroyed. But energy can change form thus as I am energy, I absolutely must go on. I visualize it as occurring in this way:

My physical body is akin to a TV set displaying the program of my life as beamed from the TV aerial from the other side of London which is my 'Soul', if you like.

I, as my physical body, am energised by a life force called the Higher Self (HS) which is analogous to the electrical current. When someone unplugs the TV and that electrical current turns off, I die (my HS leaving the body). Obviously the transmitter in London (Soul) still exists as does the electrical current (HS) but neither is now directed into the TV. My Higher Self can choose to stay as the current, unfocused and free flowing without form, for a while until it is directed to power up a new body. My Soul would then start generating the programs to be beamed through the new body (TV).

No-one knows for sure what happens to us after death and so no-one could ever prove to me that my theory is wrong and so I CHOOSE (remember the strawberry moment) to believe this and it gives me great comfort and power!

I face the fear of death head on so that I am free to live.

In some ways, it does not matter what you choose to believe happens after death as long as you choose something that allows you to release the fear of it happening. Even if you believe the lights go off and that's it, then you can take comfort in the fact that you are not going to know anything about it anyway and so release the hold death has over you and start to live.

A wonderful way to combat fear of death is to find acceptance and turn it into a real love of life. We are all dying from the moment that we are born and thus to surrender to the inevitable as soon as possible is tremendously freeing. We have enough worries to focus on with living and thus to worry about something that we cannot avoid is to waste that precious life. We are all in transition- get over it.

Surrender

Surrender is an important concept to understand because it is one of the paradoxes of life. For example, for about 30 years I wore a very precious cross for sentimental reasons and as a sign to myself of my faith in a greater power.

I then 'heard' from my Higher Self that I did not need these permission slips or tools to believe in a greater power and that I needed to be a clear channel and so I thought about taking the cross off. The thought then went out of my mind, but the next morning I was amazed to find I still had the chain on but that the cross had gone. Before I would have been very upset about this, but I just understood that the Universe was telling me that it was time to own my power without using tools.

So I told myself that I would not search for the cross, but that I would allow whoever found it to keep it. In other words, I surrendered to its loss and felt a sense of peace by letting it go. You could also say that I removed judgement about the event and outcome. I trusted. I did not allow it to become an injustice either. I merely surrendered to what is at the end of the day reality anyway and accepted that it was for the best.

Paradoxically because I had let it go, I accidentally discovered the cross that night.

To surrender to the thought of life or death being ok and trusting in that knowing will save you much pain. After all, life is just an illusion, a game and you may get to choose an even better game next time. It's the trying to control everything, to label things, to judge experiences as good or bad that also causes the suffering.

The Buddhists call this 'attachment'. I had an interesting lesson about this recently when I was teaching a meditation class and we were discussing how attachment to 'things' and outcomes causes suffering. One student stated that he was not a materialistic person and insisted that he was not attached to anything.

I noticed that he was wearing a wedding ring and I so I asked him if I could have his wedding ring. Obviously, he said no.

We agreed that the love of his wife which is what the ring symbolised for him did not exist anywhere inside the ring. The ring was merely a tool to re-energise those feelings within him. Does he need a tool to do that? The obvious answer is no. When we use material tools we are potentially giving our power away and exposing ourselves to potential suffering should the object be lost or stolen.

I believe that is why winning huge amounts of money, for example, does not often happen to people even though it might appear to be their dearest wish. If you suddenly became wealthy, the fear of the loss of that money in the future is much stronger than the desire to have it in the first place. The risks do not outweigh the gain. Fear is the strongest program running, but it is well disguised.

Again this is why we sometimes have what are known as self-sabotage programs. If we risk trying to succeed at something but fail this has the potential to cause suffering and so we stop ourselves before success comes too close!

The Buddhists believe that it is clinging, grasping and striving for things that causes of our suffering. We cling to beliefs, strive for control, and grasp at material things to make us feel secure in the world when really as creators of our reality we are in control of everything anyway. Self-acceptance, trust and faith in ourselves as creators are the antidote to this.

So I advise you to surrender and practice non attachment to everything especially things that appear to be out of your control.

Ask yourself this:

What are you attached to in life and thus fear losing? (This may be anything from relationships to emotions or material things.)

Now consider whether this attachment is healthy. Duality dictates that along with the attachment, at the other end of the 'rope' of attachment is the fear of loss. Insecurity is then inevitable. If we make our happiness dependant on external things then we are always a victim to their potential loss or removal.

The Root of Fear

Fears are at their base then are just another form of belief program. They are beliefs with negative judgements overlaid upon them. Some people, however, will maintain that they do not know why they are afraid of spiders or clowns or whatever it may be. The explanation for irrational fears mostly, and quite reasonably, lies in a scary childhood experience that has lodged in the brain and not processed as a past memory. These experiences obviously can occur in adulthood also but most times as an adult we have enough ability to rationalise events and process them properly. If the emotional experience linked to the event is extreme in the moment that it was experienced then a true phobia may be created.

Often, it is the past experienced emotional tie that is responsible for maintaining the connection to the present experiences, the undoing of which will help the individual overcome the fear or phobia. This type of fear will have developed from what is known as an initial sensitizing event (ISE). For instance, I had a fear of wasps after being stung on the hand when I was about four. This was my ISE.

Hypnotherapy works really well for these types of fears and phobias because it can access the programs within the subconscious mind and use visualisation effectively to change them.

Visualisation is the primary language of the subconscious mind. For fears with a strong emotional tie there also needs to be an intervention to remove the emotional memory often felt in the body, in addition to the work on the conscious memory of the event. Remember my 'drowning' client whose unusual action when releasing the float signalled an emotional muscle memory.

However, the other category that causes the most damage in our everyday life is fear of failure. Fear of failure is innately connected to the realm of beliefs and judgments. It may manifest in many guises like public speaking or, as I mentioned earlier, as a well hidden self-sabotage program. If you never aim for success then you never have to experience failure and the hurt that may ensue from that. It you aim for the stars and fall to earth then it is going to hurt a lot more than if you just fall from the top of a tree.

I see a lot of people in my work who have been programmed that to not succeed immediately (at a first attempt) or to not be the best at everything, automatically means that they are a failure or worthless. These people avoid all potential trials, tests or any situations where they might be evaluated or asked to compete. Consequently, they usually end up living very small and limited lives. There are lots of people out there who use many other things as rational excuses or reasons to justify not attempting something.

Often a fear can be the tool that the mind uses in order to bring to a person's attention something that the subconscious mind wants them to deal with. Let me give you an example.

I know of someone whose fear of driving covered up a very different fear. After repeated but unsuccessful steps to get driving again he discovered that there was an ISE present that had nothing to do with driving.

The fear was actually about going out in public because he had suffered a humiliating but suppressed experience in a classroom as a young child. Because he had also experienced an embarrassing incident that caused him much public humiliation when driving when he was a learner driver, these programs had become entangled in his mind.

The ISE happened to him at primary school but it was either buried too deeply or was too painful for him to face. Therefore, admitting to a fear of driving was more acceptable for his conscious mind. Because this man also had manifested mobility difficulties his fear meant that he could not go out as often as he 'thought' that he wanted to. When we discovered that the root fear was actually fear of being humiliated or embarrassed in public, he realised that his inability to drive was just another tool he used to limit his ability to go out.

If you remember from the earlier chapters, the subconscious is projecting out things that make you feel a certain way in order to grab your attention. Any fear therefore will make you feel like a victim to the thing that you are afraid of. The fear overtakes and has power over you, controlling your behaviour, if you like. And since your Higher Self knows you to be totally powerful, you will experience the negative emotion as discomfort. You are out of alignment with who you really are. Your Sat-nav system is saying 'you are going the wrong way'.

The subconscious wants you to feel 'bad' so that you will work to find the cause or root program and remove it from the computer. It is trying to help you discover what is hidden in the submerged iceberg of your subconscious mind. But because we do not understand that it is another subconscious projection, we just take steps to avoid the issue arising.

Once this man's suppressed memory of humiliation in front of his class was uncovered he was able to consciously work on the real problem. The real issue to heal was not fear of driving but not wanting to go out for fear of experiencing more public humiliation. It was in fact an issue of self-esteem.

In order to protect himself from public humiliation he had created layers of difficulty like mobility problems in order to ensure that the strongest wish – *i.e. not to risk something happening to him in public* – was constantly fulfilled. Therefore this work helped him to heal many issues that he had subconsciously been using to limit himself. Also it is essential to note that the fear of the *memory* of pain previously suffered rather than the particular subject itself that was the root of the problem.

If you can take full responsibility for all of your creations including your fears, it is possible to uncover the root problem and to remove it once and for all. Sometimes, it simply takes the time and courage to dig for the treasure.

What I would also like to point out about this story is that even though he was creating subconsciously, he was asking for something and it was being given. Because that vibration was fear based it was manifesting the desired positive outcomes through seemingly negative circumstances. He received that which he was actually (but unconsciously) asking for which was the outcome that protected him most (not to have to face the public). LOA was thus working perfectly and as we know it works just like gravity whether you know about it or not!

Fear of public humiliation is really about caring about other people's negative judgements and ultimately reflects low self-esteem. A truth that I have witnessed continually in clients is that fear can be used subconsciously as a tool to cover up a past hurt, characteristic or behaviour that the person does not want to own. And these fears are actually due to the fear of not being loved.

One of our most common fears is that we will be judged negatively, consequently be unloved and thus suffer emotional pain.

We use fear for subconscious positive reasons. This supports the philosophy of the TOUR coaching tool in that you have chosen the belief (fear) because it also has an underlying gain - even if that is to teach you something currently unknown about yourself.

If there is a particular issue or something that you do not want to do, you may project a fear of something as an avoidance ploy. If, for example, my partner wants me to go and see his family abroad every three months and I do not get on with them the next time we fly and there is turbulence then subconsciously (I am definitely not saying consciously note) I may become frightened of flying because it gives me an excuse not to go. If I cannot be assertive and tell my partner that I do not want to go, this is the perfect program of gain. None of us want to be selfish, to fail, to let others down because that will cause a negative judgement against us and result in lack of love and emotional pain!

I must reiterate strongly that in no way am I saying anyone with fears and phobias is creating them consciously. I know that fears feel very real to the person at the moment of exposure. But if we accept the idea of projection fully then the subconscious will show you that which you do not accept consciously. You will also see from the TOUR worksheets that it is your strongest belief or vibrational match that is manifesting.

Overcoming a fear also takes work on loving and accepting the self, warts and all! It is always far healthier to be honest and open about what you really want to do or not do because then you will not have to subconsciously manifest a fear, an illness or another tool in order to make yourself happy. If you are completely against doing something then at least choose to avoid doing it in a healthier way by being assertive and telling yourself that you are important too! The CORE strategy will obviously work towards achieving this outcome.

If you can accept this theory and dislodge the fear by uncovering the belief programs you will then be able to choose to create a healthier way to behave. By then creating the new ABC (action, behaviour and choice of a new belief) then your fear will ebb away because it was never the real issue in the first place. The fear is just the tool that your mind is using!

Fear of Judgement
Most of the clients that I see in my practice and classes that suffer from stress, anxiety and fear are worried about what other people think about them. They worry about how they are or will be perceived and judged in relation to how they look, what they wear, how they perform at school or work, if they are achieving goals that society values like having a good job,

having qualifications, having a partner, having children, being intelligent, blah, blah,

The list is endless about who, what and how others expect you to be. But who has the right or authority to define what is right or wrong for anyone else?

So what really is there to be afraid of? If you accept that you are the creator of your own reality then who is it that is judging/criticising you?

Ask yourself: Why would I create someone to judge or criticize me? The only reasonable possibilities are that:

A. You are trying to highlight to yourself something about whom or what you truly are; something that you do not own or something that is hiding in your shadow.

B. The situation is giving you an opportunity to practise changing, to learn about your reactions or to experience contrast that can show you what you do want.

I had a phase where 'know it all' was being thrown at me albeit in a joking way, but it made me stop and think about why I would be creating that.

I had been on a couple of courses where I was disappointed not to learn anything new and asked myself why I would create going on courses where I knew it all. Then a friend asked me about what I thought about a breathing problem and pain he had and I mentioned pleurisy. He teased about me being a 'know it all'. Coincidentally, a few days earlier, I had had a client who was fearful of being judged as a 'know it all'.

I started to realise through some other work also that the Universe was showing me that I now knew so much that I was now ready to expand my teaching and to write this book. So while some years ago that label of being a 'know it all' would have caused me real stress and heartache, now by looking at all the information I realise it was a positive message to myself. The lesson is that you are creating the people saying these things and so the message is meant in a positive way for your growth, however it may first appear.

You may recall that I covered in the chapter on LOA that emotions are there to give us feedback about our truths of who we truly are. When we feel negative emotion caused by fear and especially fear of another's judgement or criticism of us, it is because we believe that they are more powerful, knowledgeable or better in some way than us. Or we just believe that they are right and we are wrong. At the end of the day, an opinion, judgement or criticism is just a string of words that of itself has no inherent power-unless we choose to interpret the words that way.

So again allow me to reinforce the four simple CORE keys to living happily in relation to fears:

C is for Confidence

Do not fear failure. Permit yourself to make mistakes. We do not learn and grow if we are not prepared to make mistakes. There is no failure, only feedback anyway. Confidence is a magical quality that you can gain quickly and easily.

Confidence occurs when you really do not care what anyone else thinks about you. Just imagine for a moment how differently you would act, what you could do, who you would be and what you could achieve if you gave up fearing emotional pain. How would you feel if you gave up fearing the consequences of your own success? Feel the positive energy of the knowledge that you are a powerful creator in your life.

Feel the power in the fact that there is no little 'you'. There is only you as the eternal soul energy expressing in this physical form. We are all one. We are all just bags of cells and we are all more than good enough so own it!

O is for Opinion

Never fear other people's judgements and criticisms. They are simply opinion - no more and no less. You cannot please all of the people all of the time. There is not, nor am I sure will ever be, a person that absolutely everyone loves because we all like different things and so it should be. Never fear expressing who you really are or to whom you want to be.

If you find yourself fearing anyone else's judgement simply change the language to opinion and be bothered (or not) only once you have reflected. Then you may choose to change or choose to let the judgement pass. No-one else has any right to tell you how to act or to be. No-one else is ever automatically right. Also no-one can affect you unless you allow them to! Say that's just your opinion - Whatever!!

R is for Right

Ask yourself: "Is it better to be right or happy?" We waste so much of our energy and time trying to prove that we are right. Why should we be afraid of being wrong sometimes? Who cares? Caring is a sign of the ego at work. Being wrong, making mistakes or admitting in this moment you knew more than me about a particular subject does not change a thing about who you are physically, mentally or spiritually. Those things actually are a sign of positive growth and development. It really is not important most of the time. So fight battles only when it really is an important life-changing or enhancing moment. Keeping your vibration high is more important than feeling superior over other people. Be happy at all costs.

E is for Excitement

Do not fear your emotions - they are your loyal servants. Change the language from anxiety, stress or fear to excitement, thrill or exhilaration. If you stop to feel without labelling the emotions and physical sensations at the point of experiencing them then you will begin to realise that they are just sensations. It is the label that you overlay upon that feeling that makes it positive or negative. It becomes you judging the event. Is it really the fear of giving that talk at work or the excitement of a new challenge? You decide! There are no problems only exciting challenges. Do not fear change; desire and welcome the excitement that change can offer.

Emotional Labelling

On the subject of emotional labelling, let us think about anxiety and fears generally. Clients will often describe experiencing a myriad of physical symptoms and feelings. One of the things that will always help is deep breathing because this turns of the FFF system. Once you have done this for a while, let go of the labels and to just be with the sensations.

You will soon notice that there will be a change not only in the mental state but also different hormones and peptides will get released by the brain. Essentially you are coming out of the head where the troublesome thoughts are and into the body. Consciously undoing the root cause is work that can only be done at times where the anxiety level is low or fear is not present. Increasing your knowledge about the particular subject of fear and the building up of a core system of belief in yourself alongside development of trust in the processes of creation will help to allay any over-exaggerated fear.

Of course, rational analysis will also help to expose those places where fear has become so ingrained in our lives. If one has become acclimatised to that state then constant self-reflection alongside the uncovering of the negative belief programming is also vital. You can also use the CORE technique for a simple, everyday strategy and you will start to feel happier.

Now pause for a moment and see if you are experiencing another important and very common fear. Fear of change. Fear of change again is probably masking something else which is likely to be insecurity issues because we all like living in our lovely, safe comfort zones. In fact, fear of change is again a fear of loss/avoidance of pain if the change ends up being detrimental. I have seen many people who prefer to live in the misery of life rather than to try something different.

As we discussed in the early chapters, change is a natural and normal part of life. Everything is in a state of constant transformation as are we. You will have a completely new body roughly every couple of years, for example, where every single cell, hair and bone will have been transformed into a new and hopefully healthier version.

Change is good because anything that ceases motion stagnates just like water in a fish pond without a pump for example. Again surrendering to the reality that change is the only constant or that there are some things in life over which we *appear* to have no control is the only way to end suffering. Non attachment to specific outcomes also leaves open the possibility for something much better. Remember, your Higher Self is on top of the train with a much clearer and wider view than little you inside the carriage. So if the Higher Self says jump off now, it may be because she can see another train on a collision course with this one. But if you say with fear and trepidation 'oh no, I don't know where I am, I am going to stay here' you will have missed the opportunity for the much better outcome. Trust and faith in the larger 'you' are valuable tools to help you deal with fear of change. Focusing on the possibilities for a successful outcome instead of wallowing in what you fear the negative probabilities will be, keeps your vibration high and thus helps to create the outcome that you actually desire.

Why would you not always expect the best?

You think therefore you (create) matter and so it matters what you think!

Burning your boats!

There is a fabulous story I recall about a captain of a warship that sailed his ship over to an island that his soldiers needed to take control of in order to win the war. On arrival on the island, the captain ordered the burning of the boat. "How will we get back?" cried the soldiers. "We cannot and thus we win this battle and take the island or die here" the captain replied.

Sometimes, it is beneficial to burn your boats to ensure that you give something a 100% chance to succeed and thus there can be no turning back. It can be a very useful strategy. However, I would advise you to firstly search for and address any concerns or fears in the form of hidden belief programs that may affect your chances of success.

Always make an informed choice and then go for it!

A good question to ask oneself when dealing with fear of change is 'What is the worst that could happen and how could I deal with it?' Every decision has a consequence and thus to face the fear head on and have a strategy prepared is empowering. Remember, fail to prepare and you will prepare to fail.

Another good thing to remember is that just as darkness is simply the absence of light, fear can be the absence of knowledge. Do some research for evidence of other people's success with this issue: focus on how they achieved positive outcomes, the tricks they used and then model their success. Often a low level fear is merely a fear of the past by remembering a previously negative outcome or more interestingly fear of the future should *that event* occur again. But since neither the past nor future exists, both are actually fears of the thoughts around the present issue.

Both the past and the future exist only as concepts in your mind that you access in this moment of NOW. Even looking at a photograph of a past event is being accessed NOW. When you reach any point in the future it will be NOW. The only moment that exists is NOW. Therefore fears about past or future events only exist in your head and thus are actually current programs running **now**.

I say again fears are only belief programs running through your mind. Change the program and the fear will subside. Alternatively, clean up the thoughts with the TOUR and *then* face the fear gently and gradually, thereby reinforcing the new programming.

147

As Carl Jung said "One does not become enlightened by imagining figures of light but by making the darkness conscious".

Your Own Reality

I strongly believe that the media does so much damage because it constantly reports on the bad news which consequently feeds insecurity into the world at large. But the stories reported often have nothing to do with your personal reality.

Take a tragedy like the Twin Towers, for example. What really did that have to do with you? Unless you were personally involved, you knew someone who was involved or at a stretch were affected business wise by it then really it had nothing to do with your life. If there was no media coverage, no-one outside of New York, certainly internationally, would have known anything about it let alone have much knowledge of Al Qaeda. The amount of fear and hatred caused by the media frenzy and subsequent events would never have affected you. I am not in any way demeaning the tragedy of 9/11 but merely making a point about where our focus is and where it should be if we want to keep our vibration high. Compassion and care are fine and commendable to a point but over care without positive action is pointless and damaging.

So please pause for a moment and think about your local world.

Consider what you know and have experienced personally about your neighbourhood. Be sure that you are not thinking about what it is like due to the press or any other person's experiences.

For example, have you personally been a victim of a violent crime?

When I realised that a lot of my fears were unfounded, I immediately stopped watching the news. I stopped reading papers or talking as much as possible about things in the press. My personal reality was that neither I nor any of my close family or friends have been victims of crime even though all of my life I have lived in what would be regarded as a rough part of London. I then realised that I was living other people's lives or even the news editor's life and fears. These did not reflect my own truth and not only did it colour my world but it affected my vibration negatively!

Resolve to delve into the nature and validity of your *own* fears and then let go of as many as you can. Obviously a low level of awareness and sensible precautions are necessary but it is up to you to define what a reasonable, rational level of precaution is. The point is to question everything and make a conscious, informed choice about what you are doing in your life.

Do you allow people to throw their rubbish into your garden at home? Do you throw rubbish into it?

No? Then don't allow strangers to dump their rubbish in the wonderfully precious garden of *your* mind.

Take full responsibility for what you allow to be planted in the beautiful garden of your mind.

I am assuming if you have a lovely garden at home that you take care of it. You cut the grass and pull out the weeds; you plant flowers and spend time appreciating its resulting beauty, even relaxing in its beautiful surroundings. Why would you not lavish the same amount of love, care and level of discernment on the garden of your mind?

My final piece of advice to you is to set yourself one grand challenge at least once a year. I still do that and have faced many fears. When I jumped out of a plane, the fear was so great I could hardly breathe but as soon as my tandem instructor had guided us to a graceful landing I could not wait to get up there again. The feeling of empowerment was indescribable. Once you have faced your fear, you will believe that you can do anything and you can! This is often where the soul or spirit comes alive because it knows that you are capable of anything and it wants to you to achieve everything, be limitless and fly!

Chapter 13: The Tour Guides

Worksheets and meditations

"Knowing others is intelligence, knowing the self is wisdom"
Lao-tzu

In this chapter I will now present the TOUR system I have designed to help you look at conscious beliefs and fears and uncover subconscious programs that may be having an effect in your life and that may no longer be serving you.

The underlying philosophy of this work is that as we have seen, you are the problem not whoever or whatever is 'out there'. Those people and situations, fears and non-manifestations are the tools that you can use to do your work of self-discovery. Total responsibility is the key. Any other person is your creation or mirror and the negative emotion or fear is merely your guidance.

The Tour acronym is:

T - The Reality Mirror – What are you seeing? What is the problem?

O - Owning – Accept that you have created this.

U - Uncovering – Why are you choosing something that you say you do not want?

R - Reprogramming – ABC- A new Action, Behaviour and Choosing a new belief program.

Your work is to change your behaviour and your reactions. If you are the problem then you are also the solution.

This work proposes that you will always manifest whatever is your strongest belief or that you will always manifest the thing that you believe to be of the most benefit for you, consciously or not! But remember that the part of you that is responsible for choosing may be switching between the conscious Ego 'you' or the subconscious Higher Self 'you'.

You will remember from earlier in the book Freud's analogy of the iceberg as a model of how the mind is proportioned. Only a tiny percentage of the consciousness can be found above the water while the bulk of beliefs and programs exist below the surface of the water in the subconscious mind. This tool is designed to be a journey of discovery about what is below the surface of the water. It is designed to allow you to see the whole picture of any problem from all perspectives. It is also structured to uncover both root and associative programs.

In some ways, we are just like our computers that collect viruses that may slow down our systems. We often remain oblivious to them, however, until they cause serious problems.

Once you become aware of any negative beliefs, by bringing them up into consciousness you can then remove or amend them. If, however, you were to continue reinforcing them after they have become conscious to you, you would have to recognize that this was now a deliberate choice. This would beg the question of why you would want to continue to create circumstances that you say you do not want. Remember in the last chapter my friend's fear of driving was supposedly the unwanted problem! Sometimes, you will find the root is another connected, deep seated issue. All core belief programs will also have supporting programs surrounding them that may also be subconscious.

Often there are underlying positive gains to programs that at first appear obviously negative. You must write down everything that comes up and accept that it is a program and thus will be having an effect somewhere in your life.

Although you appear to deal with a single relationship or problem, the long TOUR will uncover many different programs on many different subjects so keep asking why would I choose that, what is the gain? You have to accept that if you think it and choose it–it has a gain which will be having an effect somewhere in your life. You also need to uncover the real problem, not just accept the initial idea at face value.

An example:

When I was at the worst of my depression, there was an incident where my car windscreen was smashed by a rogue golf ball. This turned out to be the last straw for me. Initially I thought the problem was the windscreen and cost, but as I eventually understood it was really about injustice and powerlessness. I thought, 'the windscreen is going to cost money that I do not have and now I will have more debt. Why does it always happen to me? Life is so unfair!' Really I was feeling powerless and a victim to events happening to me and thus acting as if I had no control. That is why it is important to write the first paragraph outlining the problem so that you can find the fundamental definitive statement which is the belief to be worked on!

The TOUR guides are presented as three long TOUR versions.

In the first, you can complete in depth analysis of any life situation, relationship or problem involving another person. In the second, you may explore beliefs and programs about specific subjects, fears, habits or patterns of behaviour. If we think of our problems as weeds in our garden of life, the long TOUR is really getting to the root and pulling it up once and for all. The short TOUR is ideal for when most of the roots are gone but there are small shoots that continue to reappear through the cracks of the paving. These too are easy to pull up if you keep on top of them. Both TOURS end with the planting of fresh positive beliefs and programs that require constant watering. The upkeep of the beautiful garden is your responsibility!

However, as previously stated in the chapter of fears, some fears or true phobias develop from a specific initial sensitising event and have a very deep emotional tie which the tools may not be really suitable for. In this case I would advise you to enlist the help of a trained professional, obviously my bias would be toward a good hypnotherapist but that is up to you.

The long TOURS particularly may bring about some emotional release, tears or anger and if this happens I would advise you to pause and just be with the emotions.

Tears cleanse, wash away pain and heal and so should never be held back in my opinion.

Once you are familiar with the nature of the process, you should be able to use the short TOUR guide and then just the acronym in order to; get quickly to the root of the problem, own it and create a new program. I have provided an easy to follow short version that will help guide you initially to uncover the programs, until you feel comfortable just using the acronym alone. I have found, however, in my trials of the worksheets that some people can go straight to using the short version and acronym so I suggest you experiment with both methods.

The TOUR allows you to discover that you are not the thoughts, beliefs and programs, but these are things that you are displaying. This is the important part of this work because you are not the personality that you have constructed with beliefs and judgements. Just as you can take clothes off the body you can remove the programs from your mind. This creates a gap between you and your beliefs and makes it easier to feel that change is possible.

In the English language, for example, we say I am angry but in other languages they say I have the feeling of anger. This separates the person from being the emotion to someone who is experiencing something called anger—there is a gap!

It is often easier to be objective and to solve everyone else's problems around you than to solve your own. This is because we are too emotionally attached to our own situations and believe that they define us. In other words when there is emotional gap, objectivity and more rational thought can occur.

I often find that students and clients resist wanting to write things down sometimes because it causes them pain to see themselves so clearly on the page. The work reveals the many layers of programming that we have. The depth of layering may depend on how depressed you feel, how much work you have done on yourself already or even how emotionally intelligent you are. There is no judgement on this because we are all on one road, some at one end and some at the other. Different techniques also suit different people. We are all unique. You should also be aware that the uncovering of supporting beliefs will continue right up until the end of the TOUR meditation in some cases.

As you find that you may now want to grow from positive things in your life, do not forget however, that you can also use the TOUR guide of positive situations to focus on and reinforce positive beliefs programs. Thus the third TOUR guide helps you to uncover the positive programming and beliefs that you have in order to maximise their potency in your life. Whilst working to develop these sheets and practising on anything I could find, I discovered that I actually created minor problems specifically with which to do my self-development work on. The majority of the self-development tools around are designed to help you deal with problems- as are mine! That is because we only want to change what is going wrong. That may seem obvious but you have to have a certain level of self-awareness in order to be strong enough to focus on the positives all of the time.

Consequently, I wanted to develop a tool that could help you work on the positive things occurring so that you can reinforce your positive strengths and characteristics! I want you to develop a powerful belief program that says 'I do my development work on all of the positive situations in my life.'

Always be courageous and brutally honest because you cannot hide from yourself –well not for long anyway. Anything that you are hiding in your shadows is eventually going to come out. My advice is to keep reinforcing to yourself that everything is just an opportunity to grow and to learn what it is that you do want and who it is that you truly want to be. If you can do that then this work will be life changing for you and soon you will be using the positive TOUR and celebrating success after success!

I have included on each TOUR guide some simple examples (see appendix) to give you an idea of how to complete it and to direct you to what sorts of things are really being asked with each question.

Once you have taken any TOUR, I would then advise you to immediately complete the TOUR of the body meditation to clear any residue and to embed the more positive program with the mental, emotional and spiritual body during the visualization.

All the TOUR meditations, worksheets and the CORE strategy are available from http://www.positivelyjoyous.com

I also advise you to watch for the evidence of change not only in that particular situation, relationship or pattern but also in other areas of your life. You may see increases in synchronicity, co-incidences or emotional peace.

Finally I advise you to then to learn and continually embed the CORE principles in your life all day every day at every opportunity. With consistent attention and focus, I believe that we can all come to a point of knowing ourselves better and thus not needing to create such tough lessons for ourselves. Your ability to understand how beliefs affect you will make such deep reflection unnecessary.

Life is supposed to be simple, stress free and exciting. The CORE principles will help you to keep your vibration high, to own and love who you are and to handle effectively in the moment anything that comes your way.

The Long Tour Guides - A general overview

Rule 1: You are not allowed to answer any questions with 'I don't know'. You absolutely do and must know the answer because you are creating the program or completing the behaviours that are causing the problem. In fact you are the only one who knows! The answer may be suppressed or well hidden in the subconscious mind, but the subconscious is a faithful servant and if you ask for the answer and wait for it to arise then it absolutely will. If you find this work challenging at first, persevere and the results will be bountiful.

The Reality Mirror

Firstly, the TOUR asks you to look into the reality mirror as that is the problem that you are currently seeing and experiencing. The TOUR then asks you to stand in the others person's shoes. This is important because that person is a reflection of qualities that exist in you and so seeing the situation through their perspective will allow you to own whatever it is that they are experiencing because that is yours to own as well!

Owning everything

In the second section, the TOUR first asks you to accept sole, unconditional responsibility for a situation. If you are new to this idea that you are totally the problem then this is likely to bring up powerful feelings and denial. All of that is great. Honour those feelings etc. Get them all out onto paper.

Uncovering the programs

Now we can deal with the situation itself. You are asked to state the problem simply in one sentence. This sums up the problem that you are creating. Then answer these questions thoughtfully as they are drawing out the positive learning about why you created this scenario.

It is giving me the opportunity to learn.........................
It is giving me the opportunity to face about myself..........
It is giving me the opportunity to practice.....................

Reprogramming

Finally, you are looking for an immediate Action to heal the specific scenario, a new general Behaviour which you then need to practice at every opportunity.

You then need to Choose a new positive belief and turn this into an affirmation about yourself to practice every day. Remember affirmations should be general with positive language, present tense and simple to remember. Short and sweet as they say!

A few suggestions would be:

I matter! - I am in control of my thoughts - I am in control of my behaviour.

Thoughts are not 'things' - I love myself unconditionally.

Everything always works out for me - I am doing the best that I can.

I am calm at all times - I can be assertive and still be lovable.

This part of the TOUR ends with a forgiveness of self for creating this problem. I like to say to myself:

"I was doing the best that I could do with the knowledge and experience that I had at that moment".

This has become a powerful and successful affirmation of forgiveness for me. If this does not feel true when you first begin saying it then ask yourself if you would be able to forgive another person who offered that explanation for their behaviour in that scenario. If it is true for them then it must be true for you as you are one.

A belief is just a thought that you keep thinking after all.

If you are still struggling with forgiveness for the self, ask yourself if your intention was to hurt the other person or deliberately cause the problem. If whatever the negative thing is that you are working on was not your intended outcome then own that. "My intentions were good" is all you can ever be responsible for once you have taken the lessons on board!

Then, there should be a moment of thanks and appreciation the other person for 'playing out' this role for you. Acknowledge that the role that other person is playing is not that of troublemaker but of a spiritual teacher who has guided you to incredible learning and evolution.

I strongly advise everyone to then complete the TOUR of the body meditation to clear emotions recorded in the spiritual, emotional and energy body. Within this meditation is the opportunity to honour the current reality, release the old and welcome in the new you.

Be aware that you will have changed simply from completing this worksheet alone and that creates another *new you* in every moment that you spent completing it.

Remember to continue this work by embedding the CORE strategy into your life every day.

The TOUR of the Body

The TOUR of the body is a visualisation/meditation which combines a range of ideas to work on clearing the negative energies on many levels.

It embeds a deep breathing technique and asks your Higher Self to help you heal and move forward. This practice requires that you bring forward the memory of the problem/situation plus any physical pain or emotion associated with the situation. The deep breathing in and out through the heart allows the heart to come into a pattern of coherence. It also calms the systems of the body.

The idea of giving the negative belief a colour aims to focus the mind on the idea of release and it helps you to see visually when that part of the work is done. By bringing to mind a really happy memory this moves the heart, body and spirit into a more positive and healthier state.

Turning up the sensory levels engages you fully with the experience.

The last visualisation focuses on the future, creating the reality that you desire and sealing it into the heart so that you can revisit it at will.

The short Tour meditation allows you to work on releasing the old and reaffirming the new belief program very quickly and succinctly.

The Worksheets

The long TOUR Guide (when another person/s is involved)

Feel free to read the user's notes before attempting to complete the worksheet. Please allow yourself the time, space and materials with which to write without limit.

1.   T - This is the problem (The reality mirror)

Look into the reality mirror and write a paragraph about what is happening 'out there'.
Do the same thing for the other person, you must stand in their shoes and see you and the situation from their perspective only.

2.   O - Own it

Own the fact that you are solely responsible creating this situation and notice how that makes you feel honestly. Write all those feelings down without censorship.

3.   U - Use it (Uncovering the belief programs)

Summarize the problem into one sentence. Then state 'I created this situation because':

It is giving me the opportunity to learn……………………….

It is giving me the opportunity to face about myself………...

It is giving me the opportunity to practice…………………….

4.   R - Reprogram (Reprogramming)

What are the 3 things that you will do NOW to embed new programs in your life? ABC

An immediate Action to take to improve the current problem in reality.

A new more general positive Behaviour to begin to practice (in life).

Choose a new positive belief (affirmation) about yourself to develop and practice (in life).

Now go to the TOUR meditation in order to complete the work

Embed the CORE principles into your life!

The Long TOUR Guide 2 - Habits, Fears, Anxiety (HFA)

Please feel free to read the user's guide before attempting to complete the worksheet. Please do not allow yourself to say 'I don't know' as an answer to any of the questions. You are the only one that knows because you are creating it!

T - The problem is (The reality mirror)

Look into the reality mirror and write a short paragraph about what is happening 'out there' when you experience this HFA. For fears and anxiety be sure to define exactly and in great detail what it is that you do not like about the object of fear.

O - Own it

Own the fact that you are solely responsible creating this situation and notice how that honestly makes you feel.

U - Use it (Uncovering the belief programs)

Summarize what the problem is in a short sentence (the belief or program)

Why am I choosing something that I say that I do not want? (Maintaining the negative HFA)

What would be the gain?

It may help to imagine having what you say you want and looking for the disadvantages of that.

I have created this HFA because:

A. It is giving me the opportunity to learn...........................

B. It is giving me the opportunity to face about myself.........

C. It is giving me the opportunity to practice.....................

R – Reprogram

What are the 3 things you will do NOW to embed new belief programs in your life?

ABC

1. An immediate Action to take to improve the current problem in reality.

2. A new positive Behaviour to begin to develop (in life).

3. Choose a new positive belief (affirmation) about yourself to develop.

Now go to the TOUR meditation in order to complete the work.

Embed the CORE principles into your life!

The Long TOUR Guide 3

Positive traits or successful situations / relationships.

1. T - The Reality Mirror

Look into the reality mirror and write a short paragraph about what is happening 'out there'. Be sure to end with all the positive emotions that you are feeling.

2. O - Own it

Own the fact that you are solely responsible creating this positive situation and notice how that honestly makes you feel.

3. U - Use it (Uncovering the belief programs)

Define in one sentence the positive Action, Belief or Behaviour

A. What is the gain in having that belief or program?

B. How can I develop this trait further?

4. R – Reprogram

Write one (at least) very general but positive affirmation that reinforces the positive belief or program that you want to develop even more in the future.

"I am…I will…I can…"

The CORE

Confidence - Do not care what anyone else thinks about you and believe that you can do anything!

Opinion - Know that anyone else's judgement about you is just their opinion. It does not mean that they are right.

Right - Question is it better to be right or happy?

Excitement - Change the labels from anxiety, stress or fear to excitement. Feel excited about this new opportunity to grow!

The Short TOUR guide

The Reality Mirror:
What is the problem that you are seeing?

Owning:
How does this creation make me feel?
What other areas in my life is this playing out?

Uncovering:
State the problem or belief.
What is the opposite belief or the solution to the problem?
Is this belief still serving you positively?
Why are you choosing something that you say that you do not want? What is the gain?
What would be a better belief to achieve this outcome?

Reprogramming:
Rewrite the new belief and affirmation.
Intend and practice a new Action, Behaviour and Choose a new belief.

Meditation

TOURING - The Body: Long version (Available as a download at http://www.positivelyjoyous.com)

Spend a few minutes on each stage.

Close your eyes and sit comfortably.

Breathe in and out over a long slow count to three through the nose (with the tummy extending on the in breath and relaxing on the out breath)

Ask for help and guidance from your Higher Self.

Bring to mind the issue and notice where you physically experience the negative emotion.

Remove any labels around this and just 'notice' the sensations as they gradually fade away.

Tune into the heart and begin to breathe in and out through the heart.

Consciously set the intention to let go of old beliefs and programming by assigning it a colour.

Breathe in positivity and joy through the heart. Breathe out and let go of the old program by allowing yourself to see the colour fading away until the out breath eventually becomes clear. Allow whatever time is necessary here.

Bring to mind your happiest memory ever and really experience it-turning up the feelings, colours, sounds, tastes and aromas. Stay with this for about two minutes.

Now spend about five minutes visualising your new belief program or affirmation taking effect and what that looks, feels and sounds like in your life. It is crucial to feel the excitement and joy of the new improved situation.

Then, seal the new positive image into the heart and return to the observation of the breath from the tummy until you feel ready to restart your new day as the new you!

Meditation

TOURING - The Body for Success (Available as a download at http://www.positivelyjoyous.com)

Spend a few minutes on each stage.

A long slow breath in, through the nose, to the count of three and then out through the nose (with the tummy extending on the in breath and relaxing on the out breath.) Locate the heart and begin to breathe in and out through the heart.

Think of the successful beliefs and programming –Assign them a colour. Breathe in positivity and joy of your success. Breathe out and reinforce the program by allowing yourself to see the colour increasing in vibrancy.

Bring to mind your happiest memory ever and really experience it-turning up the feelings, colours, sounds, tastes and aromas for about two minutes.

Now spend about five minutes really visualising your newest belief programs taking effect and what that would look, feel and sound like in your life. Feel excited and joyous about the new improved situation and outcomes. Practice your new affirmations with feeling.

Then seal the new positive image into the heart and return to the observation of the breath from the tummy until you feel ready to restart your new day as the new you.

Chapter 14: You in Relationship with You

"Do to others whatever you would like them to do to you. This is the essence of all that is taught in the law and the prophets." Matthew 7:12

In this section, I want to talk briefly about relationships from the perspective of 'oneself' as the creator of all of our personal relationships. Our relationships are really the place where we experience the most fundamental growth. We exist in relationship to everything else in our lives, but we project onto significant others in order to discover and achieve unconditional love for ourselves.

Ask yourself this: Would you like to be in a relationship 'with you?'

What sort of partner do you make? Do you behave the way you expect to be treated? Do you make the other person responsible for your happiness? Do you empty your glass to fill up the other person's or vice versa? Do you practise unconditional love for yourself and everyone around you? Do you practise self-is-ness?

I personally learned the hard way that unconditional love is a concept often misunderstood. I believed that unconditional love meant that you loved everyone else and especially your significant other despite their flaws. I thought that to be spiritual and a good person meant being loving, tolerant, patient, compassionate, unconditionally accepting and forgiving of everyone else's mistakes, quirks and behaviour. I believed that I must forgive and let go of every hurt. And I was really good at doing all those things for everyone in my life except for one person—me.

What I discovered through a very tough experience is that I count too. I matter. I am a person who deserves love, tolerance, patience, compassion, unconditional acceptance and forgiveness. If I cannot give that to myself, who is going to do it for me? I learned that it is my sole responsibility to make myself happy. But there was a time when I believed that it was my partner who was supposed to make me happy and this is the relationship that I will describe to you now.

Some years ago after returning from a Vipassana 10-day silent meditation retreat, I felt so high and peaceful it was as if I could take on the world. I made the declaration that I was going to follow the Buddhist precepts (codes for living) and at all times to be loving, tolerant, patient, compassionate, unconditionally accepting and forgiving.

I immediately found myself entangled in a relationship with a person who basically was not right for me. I want to state clearly at this point that my writing about this person may seem very negative, but that I actually take sole responsibility for creating this relationship. I will state things as I saw them at the time. However, with the knowledge I have now I understand that this person was simply a reflection of things that are also in me and thus I write with no sense of blame or ill feeling. I now consider this person to be my greatest teacher.

It is often said that love is blind. I think this is a far more profound statement than it appears. When we come into this physical world from the nonphysical, we must forget everything that we already know in order to have a truly meaningful life experience. When we enter into a deep and serious relationship we too must forget everything that we know (rationally) in order to fully experience the learning and growth from it. And in this relationship, it initially, did indeed feel like I had forgotten everything that I had learned up until that point.

Because I had set the above intentions to honour the Buddhist precepts, I ignored my own needs and wishes in order to allow my partner to fully be who he was. I continually forgave, dismissed and in some ways even encouraged and enabled unacceptable behaviour. I suffered many hurts because I was trying so hard to be that spiritual perfection that I thought I should be.

Instead of holding my own values and boundaries and keeping my vibration high, I lowered my vibration to his level. By this I mean that he was an angry, tortured soul who had suffered much hurt and pain in his life. I allowed my compassion for that pain to lower my expectations of him and his treatment of me. In short, I let his unhappy past, excuse his negative behaviour. By doing that however, I gradually understood that I was giving myself the message that I was worthless and that I did not matter.

Does that sound much like loving and accepting the self?

Most of us are susceptible not only to other people's beliefs and judgments, but also to their moods, wishes and demands. It is an assertive person with true self-love who can hold their own views, wishes and desires amongst others in the most challenging of circumstances. In LOA speak, this means being able to hold your vibration in a high frequency state despite what is going on around you.

Thankfully when I realised what I was doing, I eventually managed to take my power back and say this is unacceptable. I realised, however, that I had learned an incredible lesson about what unconditional love really meant. Note again how a seemingly negative and challenging event can actually be a pot of gold, in terms of the learning and growth that can be gleaned from it.

I learnt that unconditional love means loving *yourself* despite the conditions. It means accepting that there will be times when it is impossible to be patient, tolerant, loving or forgiving and that is ok. But most of all I learned that I could support and love this person *without staying* in a relationship with him!

We have to accept that none of us are perfect—or there would be no reason to still be here! In my opinion, the word 'perfection' should be banned from our vocabulary because perfection simply does not exist in the Universe. Nothing that nature creates is perfect or it would not have room to grow and evolve and instead would stagnate and die. Everything, especially humans, needs room to grow. The reach for perfectionism particularly in relationships often brings so much pain in our lives because it is by its very nature an impossible dream. So please if you are a perfectionist or worse still expect to find the perfect partner — give it up! Just be the best that you can be in any moment and be happy that you always do and will have more moments ahead to improve.

In my relationship, I did damage to both of us by facilitating his behaviour because I allowed him to express his more negative qualities instead of encouraging and expecting the best of him. I own completely that he was also demonstrating aspects of my character -expecting someone else to make me happy, using emotional blackmail, lying, manipulating facts to get own way etc. They were tough things to experience, but I had to ask myself if I had demonstrated those qualities anywhere in my life ever and the answer was a resounding yes-sadly. By working through that relationship not only did I get to see, own and heal those things in me, but I learned so much about myself and about relationships in general.

I am thus so thankful in some ways that I had this challenging relationship. I believe that the most difficult challenges and traumas are with hindsight the ones that bring the most learning, growth and transformation!

To be able to maintain a vibration of joy when people really want you to join in supporting their grievances or negativity is difficult but sadly is the nature of our everyday lives. Even more difficult to handle is the problem of other people's personal criticisms and judgements against us.

Mahatma Gandhi once said 'No-one can hurt me unless I allow them to' and this is the stance that one must be able to maintain in order to feel joy every day in every relationship. People only treat you the way that you allow them to and I certainly sanctioned this man's behaviour back then.

One of the best things that I learned from this experience was that if you change the label for the person that is troubling you to spiritual teacher then you see both that person and yourself differently. It changes from him/her being an aggressor and you being a victim to him/her being someone who is simply challenging you to grow.

From a LOA point of view, my partner was a man who could be so charming and full of fun but was also an insecure person who needed total control. If I had been more aware and more knowledgeable about LOA at the time, I would have kept my attention on this man's good qualities and on manifesting more of those, but I instead I focused on his negative qualities.

Think about small children. If they are behaving well, we as parents take our attention away from them. But if they misbehave, we give them all of our attention albeit in not the most healthy way. I know as a parent that I used to reward 'naughty' behaviour with attention and not praise good behaviour enough.

In this relationship, I did the same thing to some extent. The worse my partner's behaviour got or my perception of it got then the more I thought about it.

It was during this time that I remembered a very effective technique I had learned some years before meeting this man — the time honoured tradition of writing down one's feelings in letters. I used this technique and really vented in letters both to him and to myself, which once completed, I then burnt. The point here is to release anger not to cause any more pain by sending.

Writing down feelings allows the energy, emotions and anger that we sometimes hide to be expressed in a safe place. Moreover, seeing your true feelings on paper allows you to own and accept the real issues for you. Once you have taken all that learning from the letter though you must then forgive the person causing you pain, forgive yourself and burn the letter. Never be tempted to send it because this will not help either of you in any healthy way. You are the problem so do not waste your breath shouting at the mirror, it will not hear you and it cannot change what it is reflecting of you!

So often, people fail to honour their negative emotions. This is not healthy. Emotions are a natural, important part of the body.

They are a guidance system, but the energised emotions of anger and frustration also need to be released in a safe and life enhancing way. We cannot hide our angry sides away in the shadows because they will jump out at us eventually. Tears are nature's release valve for the pressure system. I explain to people who have been holding onto their pain for many years that tears are like letting out the bath water before it flows over the top of the bath. If you pull the plug out slowly, then at least the water will not flood the bathroom! I also remind them that the subconscious mind spends its whole life protecting them by hiding everything, so it is not suddenly going to give them any more than they can manage at any one time. The subconscious mind is our best friend and ally; we must acknowledge and accept our shadows throughout our lives.

As Carl Jung, the godfather of analytical psychology said:

'It must be the conscious personality, who integrates …otherwise the conscious becomes the slave of the autonomous shadow'.

The Mind/Body Connection:

There is a new field of mind/body medicine called Psychoneuroimmunology (PNI) which explores how the interactions and processes of the mind affect the physical body, the immune and nervous systems. It suggests that those who repress anger over a long period or who are unable to express their emotions openly are far more susceptible to serious diseases like cancer.

I drained my glass by giving everything to this man and by allowing him to give very little back to me. Very soon, I was empty and starting to experience physical problems. My mind could not make me see sense and so it tried to get my focus physically. I had another good example of this happening many years ago when there was a different person that was causing problems in my life. I developed a painful elbow joint that just would not heal. My wonderful and perceptive creative visualisation teacher at the time asked me who or what did I

174

want to give the elbow to in my life? I knew immediately who she was referring to and when I removed him, my elbow healed almost overnight.

The body no longer needed to reflect something that I did not understand mentally. I now understand that it is not healthy or empowering to put others' needs entirely before my own. I need to practice self-is-ness sometimes in order to refill my glass, keep healthy and be able to give.

The last thing that I learned in untangling myself from this relationship was that forgiveness is the ultimate key to happiness. I also realised that the key is always and only in my hand. Forgiveness of self-first and then of others is an essential characteristic that you must develop if you want to live a happy life. Lots of people that I meet are holding onto anger which they keep directing at others although ironically they end up the ones hurting and in pain.

Self-help guru Deborah Ford offers this exercise which I love for its poignancy and simplicity. Pause for a moment and pretend to point the finger of blame at some imaginary other and then hold your hand in a freeze frame moment. You will see that most of the fingers are pointing at you!

Holding onto anger serves no purpose. Feeling guilty about anything at all serves no purpose.

Pause again and consider this:

Does your anger or guilt change the actual situation for the better —for you?

Does your anger or guilt change the actual situation for the better —for them?

Does your anger or guilt change the actual situation for the better in any way at all?

No? Then I suggest you give yourself a break and let it go.

Look at the CORE values and examine the situation in light of them.

Ask yourself:

Am I worrying about others' judgements of me and if so, why?

Is it better to be happy or to be right?
Will I even remember this in six months' time?
Will I be bothered about this on my deathbed?

Whatever you are feeling guilty about has already happened. It is an event in the past and thus already reality. It cannot be changed. Make amends if you feel that you want to or just let the guilt go, learn your lesson and move on resolving to do better next time. That in reality is all you can do.

Repeat our mantra: 'I was doing the best that I could with the knowledge and experience that I had at that time and my intention was good'.

Often you will find that none of it really matters. Knowing this helps me to come back to the place of remembrance that life is just a game. I remind myself to stop taking it so seriously. Life is supposed to be fun after all!

I used to believe forgiveness was difficult and mostly unjust. It was like letting people off the hook. That is until it was pointed out to me that the only person suffering by my holding onto things that had already occurred, was me.

I then realised that I could forgive as a gift to myself and that this forgiveness had nothing to do with the other person. So I began forgiving everything and everyone solely for my benefit. I started practicing self-is-ness because my happiness was my number one priority. It worked a treat until I learned that as you give to others you give to yourself anyway. With my flourishing understanding of projection, I found the opening that could allow me to forgive people whole heartedly.

My heart felt advice to you therefore is in all of your relationships to practice forgiveness. Forgive them genuinely if you can and recognise that their negative aspects are in fact your own. If you can't do this, then forgive them anyway so that *you* can let go of the negative effects!

Please note, however, that forgiveness is an on-going process and that you will only have truly forgiven fully if you love that person as much as everyone else. This is the part of the process where I find that most people struggle. They can forgive someone as long as they never see that person again, but true forgiveness says: I can be with you and still love both of us, in spite of everything! Forgiveness equals the restoration of peace.

Change the way you think about that person to seeing them as a spiritual teacher and thank them for playing this role for you. Forgive yourself and laugh at yourself because you are taking yourself too seriously.

Make a clear 'note to self' which says 'I must stop taking myself so seriously.'

Another piece of advice I want to give is to never run away from a relationship or situation because you will take yourself with you wherever you run to. I advise this obviously only if things are not too damaging or unbearable for you. If possible, it is always better to face them head on and accept that this is just another thing that you can work on and benefit from in the future. An opportunity for you to practice being a better you! However, I advise you always to make an informed choice. Only stay if you can hold your vibration strongly. This again is in some ways why I stuck it out in the relationship I mentioned beforehand. I knew I needed to clear these patterns once and for all. To run away would have been akin to seeing my face growling in the mirror and running away in fear. I will see the same face in the next mirror! I also advise you to employ the LOA and keep focused on the other person's positive aspects. Easier said than done, I know!

Everything in life is practice, especially forgiveness. It is also a process and time is a great healer so forgive and forget if only for your own sense of peace. Remember that from a LOA point of view, the discord you are experiencing is the gap between you and who you really are on a grander spiritual level anyway!

I like the way animals are so loving, forgiving and non-judgemental. My lovely cat does not withhold her love because I look 'rough' on a particular day. She doesn't think I will not have that lovely snuggle because Theresa was late feeding me this morning. She immediately forgives and forgets. Our pets live in the moment, love us unconditionally and just want to play. We could all learn a lot from being more like our pets!

I have come to understand that I do not need to worry about others out there; no-one needs my help or rescuing except me! I can, to an extent be totally selfish in my aims and actions, but if I don't love myself, care about my needs or keep myself healthy, then what use am I to anyone anyway? If someone in my life appears to be ill, then my becoming unwell does not help in any way. If I can keep them focused on a positive outcome however, then I have greatly helped them.

We often criticise other people for not behaving how we expect or want them to behave. Accept that they are your blank canvas for you to work out and understand yourself in the context of that relationship.

In both of the relationships mentioned previously, I ended up working through programs that I did not know I had about my father, my hatred of men, past hurts, male authority figures, control issues etc. I now see that I had created a multi-layered and multi-faceted learning experience for myself.

In working through the lessons of my later life, I have noticed that as I have become happier and healthier in my own life then everyone else in my life has also become happier. As I have become more spiritual and self-aware so have my partners. As I have started to transform, the world around me is reflecting back a time of transformational shift. It is not, as I used to believe, that I am seeing these things and then believing. It is more that because I have a belief that I am part of everything, it obviously follows that as I am growing, all the different aspects of me are growing too.

When I heal myself and completely own and integrate aspects of me in any unhealthy relationship, eventually the problem or person disappears from my life because there is no more need for me to project out that part any longer. I have no need now to explore those aspects of myself.

Ask yourself again: Would you like to be in a relationship with you? If not, why not?

The shocking fact is that you are in a relationship with you and thus any problem is you! The problem that many of us have in romantic relationships is that we ask the other person to make us happy, but that is giving our power away and keeping us as victims.

I always explain to clients that if they can fill their glass of happiness to at least 95% before they go into a relationship and hold that amount during the relationship then they are only expecting someone else to top them up by 5%. If the new partner fails to do that or chooses to withdraw their affection, then they are still 95% complete. Holding onto the 95%, means loving yourself first, being assertive and caring for your own needs. It also means not relying on the other person in anyway.

Now I am in no way saying any of that is easy to do. However, if you understand and accept that we use all of our relationships as our main tool for challenge and growth, then nothing that occurs within them can overwhelm you or make you feel like a victim.

Taking this as your philosophy is an incredibly empowering and healthy way to be in a relationship for both parties. Would you not feel happier if your partner did not ask anything of you and took full responsibility for his/her own happiness and needs? Would we all not feel freer to enjoy each other for what we are if we didn't focus on what we could get from the other person or what they get from us?

Trying to dictate how life or your partner, children or friends must be to suit your demands is to be attached to the idea that your personal beliefs are the only way to live. In essence, it is saying that you are always right.

Peace and enlightenment arise when you accept that everything is exactly as it should be. If you can accept that whatever behaviour, view or emotion that other person is expressing is right for them (and that you have a choice about what you accept or do not accept) then you are free. The ability to stand in another's shoes and see it from their point of view is incredibly empowering. This also forms a significant part of the

TOUR work. Attachment to the idea that a person should love you in a particular way and demonstrate it in a particular way causes continuous suffering.

Ideally in relationships, we join with another person who is similar enough to us to be tolerable and yet different enough to cause us challenges. It is because of these contrasts that we will receive fabulous opportunities to grow.

If there were no challenges, no growth or jiggling up of the energy and emotions in a relationship, it would be very dull indeed. That is why we find ourselves in love-hate relationships so often.

Bliss is boring in the long term. All challenge causes growth. That's how we are —or at least how it works in my universe — bliss is boring. I need to have things that contrast from the 'sameness' of the everyday background even if that background is very good.

For example, I love chocolate. I once worked in a place where we were able to eat as much chocolate as we wanted. After the initial period of munching non-stop, I could be at work and not even give chocolate another glance. I had got bored of chocolate. It had lost its appeal as a treat. The 'specialness' of the chocolate existed only when it was something unusual, limited or new coming out of the background of the norm. After a period of having it all the time, it simply blended into the background. We acclimatise to bliss very, very quickly.

If you know everything about your partner (behaviour wise, routine wise) and nothing ever changes, that is when both of you will feel the emotional guidance coming through loudly.

It will look like frustration, boredom, irritation or maybe even hate because your Higher Self is constantly looking for the next opportunity or exciting thing to play with, to experience and evolve from.

For me, acceptance of the Buddhist tenet that everything is by its very nature impermanent is incredibly freeing. There is nothing in this Universe that is static or unchanging. As everything is energy and energy is always in motion, why should we think that our personal growth and relationships should be any different?

Anything where the energy slows to almost a stopping point eventually stagnates and dies. Therefore everything is in transition. If we accept that our romantic relationships are a place where we come together with another person for an unspecified amount of time and then naturally grow apart, we could end them more healthily I believe. Once you have learned what you needed to know or receive from that part of your psyche, it may be beneficial to move onto someone else who is reflective of the now different 'you'.

I believe that our suffering can be reflective of staying too long in a relationship that has stagnated or served its purpose from the point of view of your personal growth and challenge. But it is when we take the end of a relationship personally or see that it is a judgement upon our character that we suffer the most.

I find the Buddhist's precepts and ways of living to be the most beneficial in dealing with such suffering.

The Buddha suggested that there are four noble truths:

1. That suffering is inherent part of existence.
2. The cause of most suffering is the desire and attachment to possessions and power.
3. Suffering can be ended by detachment from craving.
4. The eight-fold path (suggestions for right living) is the means to eliminate desires and overcome the ego.

I do not agree that suffering is inevitable if one is awake in their relationships, but I do believe that most of us are still asleep. The Dalai Lama said:

"Pain is inevitable but suffering is optional," and I totally agree.

Fear of change and all the associated belief programs about age, difficulty in finding partners, not wishing to start over etc can all keep us attached and clinging onto relationships that have served their purpose. Striving to hold onto another person like a valued possession when they are clearly demonstrating that they are ready to move on also causes us pain.

I want here to make a point about soul mates. So often I meet people who are tied into relationships because they feel that the 'other' is their soul mate. Obviously you must honour whatever is going on for you personally. I am not saying that soul mates do not exist but I just want to suggest that having a soul mate in no way ties you to that person for life!

If that relationship is detrimental or becomes healed, the destiny at that stage may be for you to separate. In some ways, I believed that I had karma playing out in the detrimental relationship mentioned before and that kept me tied into it.

I once had a client in a very destructive relationship with a married man who came and went out of her live seemingly at will.

She came to me for a past life regression because she was convinced that he was her soul mate and wanted to find the tie to him. She co-operated well in the past life regression, but received no information of any value about him. She was bitterly disappointed, but I felt that actually it was the right result. For her to find what she wanted would have tied her forever to a relationship in which she was clearly suffering. I explained to her that soul mate did not mean that you stayed together for life, but really meant a relationship where deep lessons would be learned whenever the two parties incarnated together.

Thus it is imperative to remain awake and conscious within all of our relationships. It is vital to be clear about your wants and needs, to be honest *with* yourself and *open* with the other person about those wants and needs.

But be aware that you may find conflicts even between your own wants and needs. I have discovered that often I ask for contradictory things in my relationships and then wonder why my partner is unable to please me. For example, I want a hard working partner and yet I want someone to have lots of time to spend with me! I want a chivalrous, strong man who treats me like a lady, but I also want to assert, protect and demonstrate my personal power! There are many more conflicts I have and for each person they differ so I advise you to reflect on your own contradictions.

In conclusion then, always seek to be courageous and confident about whom you are within the grander scheme of life. You are after all one with the Universe. You are more than who you are in any particular relationship. You are playing out many roles just as an actor might play many roles. These roles and characters are not the real actor who takes off his costume at the end of the play.

Remember the actor within you has no need for his character to be loved by the audience. The actor is loved by his partner 'at home'. Your partner 'at home' is your eternal soul energy. When you are not in alignment with the Soul, then that is the pain that you are experiencing as the Soul knows only love for you. It is imperative to know that you are already so loved by the Universe that your glass is already full. A healthy balanced relationship should only be able to make your cup overflow!

Chapter 15: The Simple Keys to Happiness

"The weak can never forgive. Forgiveness is the attribute of the strong." Mahatma Gandhi

A Buddhist fable: The Farmer's Tale

An old farmer used a horse to till his fields. One day the horse ran away and a neighbour sympathised over his bad luck. The farmer shrugged and declared, "Good luck, bad luck? Who knows?" A week later, the horse returned with a herd of wild mares. The neighbour congratulated the farmer on his good luck. The farmer shrugged and declared, "Good luck, bad luck? Who knows?" The farmer's son attempting to train the mares then fell and broke his leg rendering him unable to work. Again his neighbour consoled him. The farmer shrugged and declared, "Good luck, bad luck? Who knows?"

A week later the army marched into town and drafted all the young men to war, but the farmer's son could not go because of his leg. When congratulated by the neighbour, the farmer shrugged, "Good luck, bad luck. Who knows?"

I love this story because it really speaks volumes about how to be happy and really sums up the simplest key to self which is non-attachment to outcomes.

The Dalai Lama in his "Paradox of our age" speech states:

"We have become long on quantity but short on quality….tall men but short character, steep profits but shallow relationships. … There is much in the window but nothing in the room"

Most people in the developed world are lucky enough to have their basic needs met. We have much quantity, but not much quality. Each individual's levels and requirement for happiness will be relative to their expectations about what is possible and perhaps probable. Let me try to demonstrate this.

Consider this: What difference would the installation of a public water tap in the street make to your happiness level?

Not much I would guess but the happiness level would go off the scale for a child in a remote and arid village in Africa.

One of the things that I advise clients who are seriously depressed and unable to think of anything good in their lives to do is to go a day without accessing clean, fresh water or electricity. When deprived of the things we take for granted, it is possible to start to see how lucky we are. I reiterate again that we are oblivious to the fact that the best and most valuable things in life like water, sunshine, love, cuddles, nature and beaches are all provided at their base freely by an abundant Universe.

Gandhi said that "The thankful heart is always closest to the riches of the Universe" and so gratitude is definitely the key.

LOA says that all you need to do is find the next best thought. No matter where you are, how depressed, how miserable, how angry with the world... the ability to simply look for something in that moment on which to focus and feel better about is guaranteed to raise your vibration—it is the law. As you focus solely on the things that you do have in your life and that you can be grateful for —eyes to read with, the sounds of bird song, beautiful sunshine—then you will draw more good things to you.

In his wonderful book "Why kindness is good for you", David Hamilton includes a wonderful quote from psychologist Robert Emmons that advises "if you want to sleep more soundly count blessings, not sheep." If you think about it, this is what traditional prayers are made of. The traditional prayer says 'that we give thanks for....' For health and happiness, it is vital to be grateful and focused on what you do have and to move the torchlight away from that which you lack. The torch is after all always in your hand.

Hamilton also proposes that acts of kindness make us happier and healthier, relieve the symptoms of depression and lead to better health. There is even a special hormone that is released whenever we hug, touch or give/receive kindness called

Oxytocin. Because of Oxytocin, the more we trust the happier, healthier and calmer we become.

I love the premise of paying things forward. "Pay it Forward" is a book by Catherine Ryan Hyde which tells the story of a young American student given an assignment about changing the world. He comes up with the idea that instead of thanking the person who does you a favour, you must do another favour for a stranger. The idea is that eventually that the original person will be the recipient of a favour, but that on its way many other people will have benefited from an original act of kindness. Small acts can change the world.

Do not complain about the world, do something about it—change your world. If you stand still, you will look out on the same scenery forever.

An inspirational student of mine was complaining that she did not like to walk in her local woods because of all the litter that had been dropped. I asked her what she could do about it and to her credit she started taking a bag with her and collecting the litter as she walked. She felt good about herself and was being the change that she wanted to see in HER world. What's more, she changed the world in greater ways because as I tell that story in my other classes and now in this book, other students have been inspired to do the same.

The one tiny decision of the original student has therefore changed the world for the better. How amazing?

So what is the first thing that you could do to change the world and when will you start? There is no time like the present and I mean that literally! There is only this moment of now in which you exist and in which to act.

Let us stop now, right now. Close your eyes and ask yourself in this moment - how do I feel? Just listen....

Being 'present' in your life:
Have you noticed that the present moment is always perfect when you stop to check? Living in the present moment is actually a learned skill, however, because most people start to

ask themselves other questions or judge things from a past or future point.

Let me try and make this a little clearer. Explain or 'show me' where the past exists.

If I ask people this, most will describe memories and photographs. Firstly, a photograph is just a fabricated creation that you can only ever access in this moment - now. You are looking or thinking about it now. Memories are thoughts and thoughts are not things. Those memories are also creations in the moment now. Where is the future? Again it only exists as thoughts and ideas that you are thinking about now. Whenever you get to tomorrow it is now. That's it—there is only now!

If you remember what we learned about reality, it only exists as far as our senses stretch and is an artificial reconstruction by the brain. Thus in any moment there is *only* what is in front of your nose now!

It is the truth that no-one can prove that you even existed yesterday because the past does not exist as a solid thing as such.

It is a mind-blower and most people immediately will reject the notion as absurd because if it were to be true it would shake the foundations of everything that they thought was real.

Is it not sad then that the only moment that exists is now and that we choose to spend most of our lives missing it, looking at the past or future or distracted in some way? Appreciation and gratitude are inextricably linked for me with being alive, being in the now and being present in the experience of the world.

So I ask you - when is it time to start living instead of just existing in a past or future worry that does not even exist?

The seconds of your life are ticking away as we speak. You can never get them back again.

You will never be the same you ever again.

Let's say that you walk to the station every day to catch the train for work and that walk takes 20 minutes, twice a day. Over a working week (five days) you have spent 3hrs and 20 minutes of life walking to and from work. Most people that I see walking along these days are distracted by headphones or mobiles. Most are usually rushing or have their heads down so as to avoid anyone else's gaze or social interactions.

When the Buddha became enlightened after meditating under the Bodhi tree, one of the things he saw was that he had spent all of his past lives running from A to B to C.

What he realised was that he had spent his lives focused on arrival points and had missed all the living that took place on the journey between these points. This is exactly what our aforementioned commuters are doing.

So often we are focused on the end point of a task that we miss the bliss of the journey —in this scenario, 3 hours and 20 minutes of beautiful gardens, smiling, making eye contact with others, the sensations of the wind on your face or the sunshine on your arms etc. If your attention is not focused in the moment you can miss lots of precious moments that will never, ever appear again. Every single minute missed whilst we are entranced in distraction is a minute wasted. If a task becomes routine and we can do it unconsciously, we tend to zone out and miss being in the moment.

The term for being totally in the moment in full sensory awareness is called 'mindfulness' and it is an amazing way to live your life.

Research shows when people have near death experiences many of them have a new and refreshed view of the world, of nature and of the beauty that surrounds them. Once people really start to get into meditation as a way of life then the natural world of animals, birds, insects and nature comes alive to them - it's as if they wake up and open their eyes for the first time. They really start to see and the colours become more vibrant

"Go inside and know thyself" as Buddha said, but you must also look outside to know thyself in relationship with the glorious, vibrant world that you have created too.

A student of mine went to a funeral where in the eulogy it was pointed out that all of your life exists in the gap. What the

Celebrant so poignantly referred to was the hyphen between the date of birth and the date of death that one could see on the order of service card.

Living is now, in the gap, that's all there is, this moment, this precious once in a lifetime never to be repeated moment of now. You will never be this person in this place at this time with this opportunity again. Do not run from birth to death always trying to get somewhere or to achieve something. Be present, be aware and be awake. Never forget that you are a human being! Living in the now means *being* rather than doing. It means if you are performing an action or a task, being present in the sensations of doing that task. You have chosen to be in a physical environment because you want to experience the sensations of life. Why would you come from a nonphysical environment and be born into a physical environment if it were not simply for those wonderful sensory experiences that one can only have via a physical body?

I am a big fan of the concept of meditation as your whole life. Yes, of course there is huge benefit to be had from sitting and quietening the mind in formal practice or from contemplation of the self, guided visualisation or any of the other formal meditative practices. However, meditation as life can enhance the quality of the experience of your life beyond measure.

Walking slowly and mindfully to the station, looking at the beauty of people's gardens, stopping to smell the flowers or daring to smile at everyone will allow you to live that 20 minutes in joy and happiness. Sometimes it is just nice to walk rather than run! You will arrive at the station feeling very different than if you rushed there and arrived stressed, hot and bothered or in a daze.

Training yourself to learn how to breathe a healthy, deep breath will do wonders to help your health and stress levels. Remember being in a long-term state of stress will not allow the body to heal and repair. The Institute of Heart Maths has done amazing studies about how the heart goes into a pattern of chaos when someone merely watches the news, for example!

Meditation in its purest form teaches one just to sit and observe the breath. There is nothing better to bring you into the present moment than this.

You can practice efficient breathing whilst you are washing up, ironing, photocopying, watering the garden, moving, sitting, standing at the bus stop etc. You can practice mindfulness and being present in these tasks and many others. How does the water feel and move around your hands when washing up? What are the sounds like? When does your hand decide to move and can you become aware of where that movement starts? Who makes that decision? Washing up is a full on sensory experience if you allow it to be!

Your life *is* the washing up not at the completion point of it!

If you have to wash up every day, is it not better to do it with joy? (Note to my son!)

Any task where there is an element of stillness or a repetitive pattern that would normally send the conscious mind wandering off can become a wonderful experience.

I have my best contemplations doing mundane tasks. (Obviously you must always be fully present when driving or operating machinery!).

Jean Jacques Rousseau said "Things do not change, we change" and so in honour of this, here are some very easy suggestions to bring you into the present. If you do them they will transform the way you feel very quickly:

Practice efficient breathing. (How to do this is explained later in the meditation chapter)

See everything as if it were the very first time that you saw it.

Bend down and look at something from a child's eye view.

Stop and really analyse the intricate design and detail of a flower or of your hand.

Listen to nature or to the silence between the sounds.

Eat slowly and with awareness. Really smell, taste and experience the textures of every bite. Be honest - how much of what you eat normally do you even taste?

Slow down and listen to your loved one or child with 100% attention.

Slow down and listen with your eyes and ears.

Stop every now and again. Take a deep, long, slow breath and ask yourself, 'could this moment be any better?' Literally, just this moment. Whenever I have done this exercise, I have never experienced a moment that needed anything else. In that moment I am and that is all I need.

Smile at everyone that you meet without judgement.

Give everyone the benefit of the doubt.

Choose to believe the best in everyone.

Trust that as everyone is you and that they are trustworthy.

See your world as a safe place.

Keep your head up, your eyes open and your body language open and welcoming to all.

It is your world, take responsibility for it. As Buddha said:

"It is better to light the smallest light than to complain about the darkness."

Lao Tzu said: "A journey of a thousand miles must begin with a first step." and that is so true. Just put one foot in front of the other and you will eventually arrive at your destination. Life is much simpler than we want to make it. It is a game, a dream or an illusion. Not sweating the small stuff is the simple key to a happy life.

Be grateful that you get to play the game. Be grateful that you have designed it so well. Be grateful that you get to be God, the creator of your own world. There is always something to be grateful for in every single minute of every single day!

I felt strongly that I wanted to reiterate these points because in truth unconditional self-love and acceptance is one of the most important things that we all really are here for and trying to learn to express.

When I tell people that they need to be self-is, most baulk at the thought. Lots of our early programming will have put the belief that it is wrong to be selfish strongly in the mind. But this is only an unquestioned and limiting belief that I for one have proved to my own satisfaction to be wrong!

Now I must repeat again that I am not advocating hurting anyone else nor taking anything from anyone else but I am advocating loving yourself first. You are not here to suffer for anyone else and certainly not to live anyone else's life and beliefs. Self-is-ness is the key.

Allow the belief that everyone is on their own journey and is empowered enough to make their own decisions, choices and mistakes. This is particularly the case for our children. We think we are good parents if we tell them what they should or should not do, but in our efforts to guide them we are actually making them follow our beliefs and values. All that happens is that they end up living our lives and resenting it!

So let us bring all this learning together now.

When asked what was wrong with the world, the English writer G.K. Chesterton wrote "I am".

What you truly think about your world and yourself, you will face in every relationship and every event. When you can love, accept and respect yourself fully, the ability to respect the other fully can only result in harmony.

Remember that you are always in a relationship with your Soul too .When you feel the love for yourself in all the forms in which you experience creation 'out there', the alignment that you experience will feel like joy and love and bliss. Be self-reflective, question everything, create your day and review your creation at the end of the day with a heart full of gratitude and a desire for more.

To be, do and have more is your birth right especially when it comes to love.

Love is all there is. Love is all there is of you!

If you do not love you, who else can or will?

If you don't think you are worth it, why should I?

Chapter 16: Meditation - Pure and Simple

"Happiness is reached when a person is ready to be what he is" Desiderius Erasmus

I believe that meditation is an essential key to unlocking the door to a healthy mind, body and spirit and for this reason I really want to honour its place within this work and our lives. As I said at the beginning of this book, it is vitally important for us not only to do our work uncovering beliefs and programs, but also to recognise that the mind and the body are two parts of the same thing. They are intricately connected and in a constant state of interplay. They exist in a complex relationship that must be addressed because thoughts, traumas and energy are recorded and held within the muscles and energy pathways of the body.

Another reason to meditate is because you exist in an intricately divine relationship with your Higher Self and Soul which must be honoured and nurtured. For me, this is done in the quiet of meditation when the channels are open, dedicated and clear. The practice of certain meditation techniques can also raise your personal vibration and happiness set point.

When people first experience meditation in my classes, they often have a sudden release of emotions and cry. I always ask them to stay with this and to recognise that if their emotions are that close to the surface then they are ready to be healed.

As stated previously, tears are a natural release mechanism. I usually find these are the people who will readily tell me how their heads are so full that they cannot switch off.

Our modern day lives are so full of technology and all kinds of other distraction. The constant mind chatter and distractions are the tools that we use to avoid meeting ourselves. Inside the meditation space, at the first opportunity that it gets the Higher Self will want to grab the attention of its host. I always imagine the Higher Self sitting on top of the train, suddenly finding that the train has stopped and the individual has removed their headphones. She now begins dangling down outside the window and knocking loudly to be let in! Let her in because she has a magical story to tell you about what she knows from sitting on top with a panoramic view!

For me, the most joyful and exciting aspect of meditation is that it provides a doorway to tap into new knowledge and consciousness. It is spiritual. It is the connection of all things where the body can disappear and you can feel that you are one with the universe and one with everything. It is the place that you can really experience yourself as spirit- u- and- all. Meditation is a very right brained activity in so far as it uses the powerful subconscious mind and creative imagination. Visualisation techniques particularly can be employed to seed the future, rehearse future outcomes and bring the wanted into the now. It is also extremely powerful for healing.

Going into the silence connects you to the now or present because there is nothing left to judge or measure the flow of time against. By the silence, I mean being away from all distractions. This usually means a retreat of some kind. During a retreat, one does not talk at all for a specific number of days so that the left hemisphere where language dominates rests and the right hemisphere where the Higher Self resides can come alive. In the silence there is only 'what is' and thus no recognition of 'what is not' because there is no contrast to be found.

There are no distractions, labels, striving or reliance on anything other than the self which is incredibly empowering. In the silence you meet the self.

If you listen to the silence even at home, you will actually find that you can tune into ever increasing levels of vibration or tones that start with Om which is traditionally thought of as the sound of the Universe. But more than that and for me particularly it is the purest place of focus, connection and is believed to be the highest vibrational state. As we know from the Law of Attraction, it is vitally important to keep your vibrational state as high and positive as possible if you want to experience true joy and be in that high flying state.

Unfortunately, I feel meditation is often sorely misunderstood. If it helps, you can call it relaxation, time out, self-hypnosis or anything else- they are only labels after all. There are many different types of meditation, each with their own intent and outcome, and it is worth trying several to see what is right for you before giving up on it entirely.

In some ways, all of life is meditation and it is the most natural state that you could find yourself in.

I chose the phrase 'all of life is meditation or it is the most natural state you could find yourself in' carefully because you are already 'meditating 'a lot more than you think. Day dreaming, imagining, listening to music, contemplation, waiting, sunbathing, washing up, walking in nature – these can all be activities where the conscious mind is out of the way and the peacefulness of a quietened mind can prevail.

In its most basic form, meditation is really a place where the chattering mind can be quietened by an alternative focus which then allows inner peace to arise. Traditionally that focus is the breath, a chant or a flame, but it doesn't have to be that way!

It is a common misconception in meditation that you are trying to stop all thoughts and that is not technically true. The Buddhists refer to the chattering mind as the monkey mind. In this analogy, the mind is inhabited by a monkey swinging from tree to tree, forever active and at work. The monkey represents the thoughts and distractions. Through meditation it is your job to take control of or train your monkey!

Some practitioners of meditation use a host of tools and permission slips to aid good practice such as bells, bowls, mantras and beads. Different religions for many years have embedded rituals and rites as permission slips to aid practice. I make no judgement other than to say I prefer to keep it simple and clean so that I can meditate anywhere and at any time. I suggest always owning your power and being self-reliant but as with everything it is entirely your choice.

195

You can even think of meditation as conscious sleep because 20 minutes of meditation in the morning is worth two to three hours of extra sleep I find. After my morning meditation, I feel so energised, clear headed and ready for the day ahead.

I even tell my students to set their alarm 10 minutes earlier so they create extra time for meditation. Doing this not only starts the day off on a good vibratory note, but also embeds mediation firmly into your morning routine.

As we know, the heart is a powerful component of creating your reality and including it in your meditation and/or visualisation will bring about your heart's desires! To send out love and healing from the heart is also sending that through the field to take effect in your reality. There is a powerful Buddhist meditation called The Metta Bhavana (meditation of loving-kindness) which is a practice of sending your loving kindness to all people. I feel that it is more powerful to embed sending that kindness through the heart. As everything is one and connected, there is no doubt that your intentions will have a wonderful effect in reality.

There have been countless studies about the power of prayer and healing which make sense if we are all connected.

This connection is via the electromagnetic or energy field. The IHM have also now have proved that there is evidence of organized energetic communication through the field. Using equipment to measure heart and brain waves, they have even proven that heart field of one person can affect the brainwaves of another particularly when two people are close to each other.

Research conducted at the Institute of Noetic Sciences (IONS) has shown that if a wife, for example, thinks of her husband who may be many miles away in a sealed faraday cage (which eliminates any opportunity for electromagnetic interference, communication or cheating) the thought can be recorded instantaneously in the brain pattern of the husband. This is true even though he may not be consciously aware of his wife thinking about him. This confirms that we are all connected. Everything is embedded within everything else.

It is interesting to pause here for a moment to reflect on the fact that science is now mirroring what most religions propose. This is that we are all indeed one and interconnected energetically, spiritually and by karma. Energy and information flowing through your heart's energy field is transmitted through your body and brain. This energy then interacts with other people, as well as communicating your internal state to the environment.

I have learned through my knowledge of the power of the heart that the inclusion of the heart in meditation is paramount. Breathing in and out from the heart brings it into a coherent pattern which is excellent for good health—lowering the blood pressure —but also for increasing your intuitive abilities.

Meditation also allows you to tune into the body and to start to know it fully. It is akin to women being advised to examine their breasts so that they become familiar with the 'regular' lumps and bumps. This then enables them to catch any irregular anomalies quicker. The more you are tuned into your body's norm, the earlier you can pick up any changes.

The mind and body are one incredibly intelligent holistic system of which it is important to increase your knowledge and awareness. It speaks to you and reflects your thoughts just as clearly as the reality mirror. The traditional meditative techniques of awareness, mindfulness, self-witnessing and conscious breathing can help you to develop the principles of moral responsibility, compassion and connectedness. The health benefits of meditation range from better sleep, improved movement, lower blood pressure, improved memory and concentration and increased serotonin levels. The endorphin serotonin promotes healthy, normal communication between the emotional and rational brain, but emotions such as anger burn up serotonin very quickly. Meditation can also increase grey matter in the brain.

I am now going to give you a guide to basic meditation practice.

My advice as always is to keep it simple and to remember that although meditation is a natural state, it may take some practice to settle down the mind. The mind can and should be a faithful servant.

We can easily train it to perform differently, but we must allow it time to change. Remove all judgements and expectations around time. If you only manage 10 seconds of peace and non-thought - how fabulous! Celebrate that 10 seconds and look forward to making it 20.

Please do not feel that you have to strive for any particular outcome as this striving in itself can cause a block of energy and frustration. Practice detachment from all expectations and outcomes. Simply meditate for peace and calm, but remain open to receiving higher energies.

For me, learning to meditate initially is about allowing you to take time out simply to breathe and be calm. The first training that you need to do is just to be able to maintain your focus on the breath for a very short period of time.

Basic Meditation Practice

Let us now begin. (Please note that if you prefer to be guided through this meditation practice, you can download a recording of it on my website http://www.positivelyjoyous.com)

Firstly, find a comfortable place where you will not be disturbed. Close the eyes.

Breathe in and out through the nose. Over a long slow count of three, breathe in and allow the tummy to extend out. Then breathe out, again to a count of three, and allow the tummy to relax. This is the way babies breathe naturally. Do not get too wrapped up in the mechanics of the technique, just set an intention to breathe slower and from a deeper place.

Listen to and feel the breath. Follow its rise and fall. Allow it to be a full sensory experience. If you are concentrating solely on all these aspects of the breath, no trivial thoughts should enter the mind at least for a while.

If your mind does wander, here are a few techniques that can help.

1. Acknowledge the thought and then place it on a cloud and watch it float away. Return immediately to the observation of the breath.

2. Acknowledge the thought and then with the eyes closed and the head still, look slowly to the left then to the right, then again to the left and then to the right. Then return to the observation of the breath.

3. Allow the thoughts to flow across your mind like a film. Notice them but don't engage in them. Return to the observation of the breath when you are ready.

Keep it relaxed and accept that some days will be more successful than others. Do not have any expectations and do not allow yourself any limiting programs such as "I can't stop my thoughts." "I can't sit still." Explore them and preferably drop them. If you can't drop them then at least add YET to the end of the sentence.

Now finally let us perform this practice again.

Take a moment to look around you. Now one by one, remove all of the labels of the objects that surround you.
What is left if you remove the labels of book, hands, you, chair, room, house, etc?
Take away the labels and there remains All That Is.
Remove the labels and where do I end and you begin?
We are all one.
What is left is no-thing but everything.
It leaves one thing – energy.
Everyone is me, everything is me, and everything is God or the Universe coming to know itself through the mirror of its own creation.
Know that you are God. Know that you are the whole Universe expressing through this vehicle. Most importantly of all, know that you are valuable to existence and that you are worthy. You are always good enough.
Treat yourself as you would God and love everyone as you do yourself!

Conclusion

"I think therefore I 'matter' and so it matters what I think".

"I am doing the best that I can do with the knowledge and experience that I have in this moment and my intentions are always good".

Whilst on a recent silent retreat at The Seekers Trust in Kent I did a wonderful meditation in their beautiful rose garden. As I did so, something suddenly shifted inside of me and I realised that that garden was the best of what was inside of me or of my mind. The beautiful colours, the peace, the roses, the plush, vibrant greenery which to me symbolises love and health...they were all in my reality mirror and therefore a true reflection of me in that moment of time.

A mirror is simply a neutral, honest reflection of the picture that is presented before it. So at that moment I realized that I must have been an actual element of the garden to be seeing that reflection of me! I was the garden literally. There was no separation. I was in the being state of a garden—peace, beauty, growth and tranquillity. I was totally in the now. If my life is a faithful physical mirror to me then the garden must be what I 'looked' like if I could see myself on the other side of the mirror so to speak. This for me was absolutely a defining moment in my life.

In that moment, I understood what it really means to claim that we are 'All That Is' as a state of being rather than as a concept! I also finally understood what Gandhi meant: I have to be whatever I want to see in the world because it is simply a neutral mirror! I finally knew on an experiential level that which I knew 'mentally' before. If I want my reality to become abundant then I have to be the essence of 'abundance' now!

The world is me and I am the world. The world is my sensory data, my perception of it and my relationship to it. I do not go out into the world; the world goes out from me.

I hope that during our precious time together I have sown the seed of, and nurtured a realisation of your eternal soul energy. If not, I have faith that I will have at least planted some seeds of change for your future cultivation.

I have written this book to help awaken you to your full potential as gently and yet as firmly as I can. I hope that I have successfully reminded you that not only are you the creator and the created, but also all of your creations. I also want to remind you that life in some ways is very simple but we allow it to become too complex by worrying about things that are unchangeable, not our business or simply not adding to our joy. You now have all the tools and skills to create positively if you choose to focus on that aim.

I have a tool box sitting under my stairs at home with a tool for every type of problem. If I leave that tool box under the stairs whilst the house crumbles around me, that is clearly my choice. The old adage 'You can lead a horse to water, but you cannot make it drink' is relevant here. I have offered you many tips, ideas and techniques, but if you do not actually use them then they cannot repair your problems!

You can achieve amazing things in your world by thought and intention. There is no work to be done 'out there' as such. Free will is power. Choice is power. To be awake and conscious is the greatest power. Inside you somewhere you already know this, just as the tiny cell inside the little toe knows intuitively that it is part of something greater.

So please take responsibility for your choices and make them consciously and deliberately. Do not allow yourself to sleepwalk through life with your thoughts leading you blindly. Wake up and join in this potentially exciting joyride.

You can be, do or have anything — this is not just some tired old axiom.

It is in fact the key to creative success because if you can embed that belief program into the mind and hold your vibration to it, you *will* create miracles.

What you will experience in your creation is purely the sum of the beliefs that are operating in your mind.

I am after all merely the sum of all my judgements about myself and how I experience *my life* is the sum of *my* judgements about it.

Look around at your life and if you are happy with it then fabulous, but if you are not- do not try to wash the face in the mirror – wash your own face!

Life is meaningless in that there is nothing that you have to do. There is no God laying down the law of how you should behave, achieve or think otherwise the concept of free will would become a redundant farce. However, alongside the acceptance of free will as a fundamental tenet of reality comes the realisation that fairness, equality and justice cannot exist. Yes, we can ask for rules and laws that make a cohesive and safe society, but anyone is free to choose not to follow those rules, to treat you unfairly or to have their own ideas of justice. Acceptance of this tenet is the secret to peace!

It is all about doing what makes you happy. Every single thing that you experience fills in another tiny piece of the jigsaw of the Universe. You have been created as a perfect jigsaw piece. You fit perfectly and if you did not the jigsaw would never be complete. Every event and person involved within the universe is unique, significant and valid. Your worth was established at the very first moment of creation.

Notice that everyone and everything brings you service in some way. Be grateful for that. As you do unto others you are doing to yourself literally. As you give, you receive 10 fold back as really you just gave it to yourself anyway. So love everyone, be kind to everyone but most importantly love yourself unconditionally because without that you have no love to give.

Practice Self-Is-Ness. Keep your vibration high, focus on the positives and bring everyone else up with you. There is no work to be done out there because there is no-thing out there. You are indeed spiritual - Spirit-You and All.

There is only you looking in the mirror and staring back at you is God in all 'its' beautiful glory.

I would like to end this book with the rest of my story because in the months it has taken me to express my ideas through this work, I have grown exponentially. (If you want to know yourself better, write a book!). Creating this work has been an amazing journey through the recesses of my mind. I believe that I have undergone a transformational shift through this process which has in some way attuned me to a greater knowledge. I have used it as a tool to remind myself that I am so much more than I thought I was. I am now willing to accept my power.

What I realised some months after deciding on the Tour as a theme is that I am the best person to write this book, the best guide for your tour, as I myself have undergone the journey from deep depression to amazing bliss. I hope that I have shown you the route, the highlights, the history and the points of interest throughout this journey and finally have been able to answer all of your questions.

I can see this clearly in my life because as I have changed so has the world and my students. It is true that the more people that I teach, the more teachers that I create and therefore can learn from. Additionally, the more varied and changing mix of people that I meet, the more reflections and opportunities to practice seeing and owning *my* beliefs, I receive.

If you read this book again a year later, you will notice that you have a very different experience of it. You will create the message that you need from it at any given time. It may even appear as if you have never read it before.

I have that experience all the time because I have a belief program that God speaks to me through books and so it is!

There may be a grand purpose for you or there may not be a grand purpose for you. You may want to believe that you are here for the joyride.

Either way, these are just belief programs so pick the one that works best for you. Be courageous and choose to follow your excitement because fears can only ever make sense if you believe that something outside of you is responsible for creating your life!

There is plenty of time, all the time in the world in fact. It's all a work in progress. It's all about the journey; life is in the gap.

I can definitely say that manifesting the life you desire is a truly empowering way to live and miraculously, it is always you that get to decide who holds the bag of truth.

It is your turn now to change the world. Pass this book to someone who you believe would benefit from reading it. Pay it forward if not with the book then with the knowledge. The more people that you teach, the more teachers there will be around you.

Change yourself for the better and the world around you will reflect that change.

Finally, the bottom line:

What will you regret most on your death bed?

One of the most common regrets of the dying are reportedly that people wished that they had lived lives that honoured their own expression of happiness rather than fit into other people's expectations. They wished they had worked less and been more emotionally open and expressive. They regret most often what they haven't done rather than berating themselves for what they did do. And finally they wished that they had given more time and attention to friends, family and the simpler things in life.

"Most men die with their music still within them," stated Ralph Waldo Emerson American essayist and poet.

Don't let any of that be you!

This is a time of immense transition for our world.

Live, love and always be positively joyous - until we meet again!

Appendix - Example Worksheet
Long TOUR guide - with another person(s).

This is a sheet that I completed regarding an incident involving a person where I felt disappointed in myself and angry with her. I have changed the names for anonymity.

Scenario: We had gone away for the weekend and Tricia had had car trouble on the journey down.

We had stopped at a friend's house who was a mechanic and he told her it was a problem with the exhaust box crumbling and blocking the exhaust. I was the one that offered to go with her to the local garage to get it fixed whilst the others went to our destination in the other vehicle.

The first garage said it was a different problem and sent us to another garage. The 2nd garage said the exhaust box only needed sealing and the radiator needed a new cap but we would have to leave it there over the weekend which we did.

Money was a big issue for Tricia and obviously neither of us are mechanics. Thus I advised her to just get the basics done here and get someone to look more closely at the problem when we got back home.

When she collected the car on the Monday it was still playing up. Tricia was crying and panicking about getting home safely, driving it on the motorway and blaming me because I had advised her to do the basics!

1. The problem is (The reality mirror)

ME: Tricia is so ungrateful as I was the only one that offered to go with her. It's so embarrassing her acting like a little kid screaming and crying at the top of her voice. I am seeing her red, angry and crying, rushing around, she can't work the phone. She's shouting accusations and not taking any responsibility for the situation. She's a grown adult and should have made her own mind up. I was just trying to help. Don't know why bother! My heart is racing with building anger and frustration at her over reacting and not listening to reason. I shouted at her to grow up and stop blaming others. I feel angry, frustrated, helpless, guilty, impatient and sorry for her, disappointed that I reacted.

TRICIA: Why does this always happen to me? Everything always goes wrong for me, it's her fault, she told me to do it, and I knew I should have gone with my gut instinct. How am I going to get home? I can't drive on the motorway like that, you can't trust garages, no-one wants to help me, it's alright for them, I won't get home til eight if I'm lucky.

I feel angry, frustrated, scared, and fed up, cheated, impatient, stupid and helpless.

2. Own it:

I feel sorry that I have projected this on to her and caused this problem for myself. I feel responsible for advising her wrongly although the intention was good. I caused it somewhat by rushing her into that, doing things on the cheap (poverty consciousness again!) and it shows that I still don't believe fully that I can hold my vibration when with family.

The emotions that I was experiencing within it are clearly matching hers. However, I also saw that that is how I used to feel all the time when I was depressed and everything would go wrong for me. I would use exactly those phrases! I remember the feeling of it all being out of my control. Thus I have created this scenario because for a few years now I have believed that she is the past version of me and I try to help her in order to heal past hurts in me. She is also bringing up my shadows.

I also see that this is a repeating old belief pattern where if I do something good for someone it somehow ends up going wrong.

Finally, as family is the only place left in my life where I struggle to maintain my vibration this is also a current theme that needs changing.

3. Use it (Uncovering beliefs and programs)

The problem is that: I can't hold my vibration high when with my family.

It is an opportunity to learn: That I can spend time with my family and keep my vibration strong, that I do not have to do my development work through negative examples, that I can be who I truly am in their company, that I am a good person, that I have come so far, that you never get this work completed!

I am facing about myself: All the negative qualities and emotions revealed in section 1 and 2 need to be honoured or adapted to be powerful forces in my life, that there is still work to be done, that I am not always right.

I am practising: Holding my vibration strong in the face of all circumstances.

4. Re-program

A. Action: I will apologise to Tricia and make up.

B. Behaviour: I will step back and allow others to make their own decisions.

C. Choosing new belief: I matter positively in all my relationships.

Summary

The CORE strategy would have helped me: have the confidence to hold my vibration through this stress, to dismiss her judgement of me as opinion and not rise to her bait, to be quiet and be happy rather than fight back to be right and finally to care more about my overall happiness rather than allowing myself an opportunity to vent unnecessary anger!!

When I did the TOUR meditation to clear this, a new belief came up which said that I love spending precious quality time with them all and then the strong realization surfaced that I really do not want to ruin what are usually fun occasions.

I set the intention that fun experiences and quality time with them is more important than working on me. I felt a huge shift as I let go of the old programs represented by the black smoke.

Thus, it is vitally important to realise that the discoveries and uncovering will continue right up until the end of the TOUR meditation and may even continue to process over the following few days of your life!

Long TOUR Guide - Fear of Spiders

1. The problem is (The reality mirror)

When I see a spider I want to run away. I hate their big furry legs. It's the look of them creeping or running so fast. I know they can't hurt me but it's just the look of them. I panic and have to run out of the room. I'm better with small ones now. I have always felt like this so I don't know where it started. Hate them! I want to stop it because I feel it's pathetic now I know they can't hurt me. I feel scared, my heart races and sweaty palms, I feel pathetic.

2. Own it

I feel pathetic, weak and stupid but if I am the problem then I am the solution.

3. Use it (Uncovering the belief program)

The problem is that: I am scared of spiders, which makes me feel pathetic and stupid.

I am choosing this problem program because then no-one will expect anything from me, I don't want to have any responsibility in life and then I cannot fail and let people down.

Here the person has discovered that the fear of spiders is not the real problem. The fear was the tool that was achieving the avoidance of the real underlying problem which is the fear of letting others down. There is obviously good work to do around developing the CORE belief system particularly around confidence, self-esteem and judgements of others!

You can clearly see how the fear of spiders is the tool in which he is trying to show himself that he has a belief program that he is pathetic and stupid and thus plays that out in reality.

Believing is seeing. If he starts to believe that he is in control, can handle responsibility and is good enough he will no longer need the fear of spiders because he will have got the message and moved on!

I have created this to learn that: I have self-esteem issues.

It is an opportunity to face: I do not want to accept responsibility.

It is an opportunity to practice: being strong successful and confident.

4. Reprogram

Action - I will face my fears head on and remove the next spider I see from my room.

Behaviour - I will accept more responsibility for myself.

Choice - I choose to believe that 'I am good enough.'

Thus it is vitally important to accept that the realizations and uncovering will continue right up until the end of the TOUR meditation and may even continue to process over the following few days of your life.

The Long TOUR Guide –
Positive Traits or Successful Situations/Relationships:

This sheet was completed after a person dealt successfully with a colleague at work that was undermining her and taking advantage of her conscientiousness.

1. The successful change was (The reality mirror)

I was really pleased because I stood up to Leila and asserted what I wanted, instead of curtailing to what she thought that I should do. I used all the tools that I had learned about saying no, knowing that we all are as good as each other and that my happiness is important too! I felt that I was completely fair. It really felt good to feel confident even though I was shaking inside. I know now that I can do that in future too.

2. Own it

I really proved to myself that I could do it and it feels so empowering to know and prove to myself that I create my own reality. I see that I now need to stand up for myself with my partner who is taking advantage of my generosity and not pulling his weight or treating me well. I learned that people actually like it if you challenge them in the right way and are fair.

3. Use it (Uncovering the belief programs)

Define in one sentence the positive Action, Belief or Behaviour.
I'm growing, loving my changes, being assertive, coming out of my shell.

A. What is the gain in having that belief or program?

All of my personal development work is starting to take effect and I am seeing that I am the creator of my reality and I do matter.

B. How can I develop this trait further?

I am going to keep doing courses and looking for opportunities to practice being me!

4. Reprogram

A. Action: I will ask for more training and responsibility in my next appraisal.

B. Behaviour: I will be assertive and courteous in all situations.

C. Choose to believe: I am good enough.

Now I will reinforce the CORE strategy into my life and complete the TOUR for success to further embed this success on a body and spirit level.

Bibliography

P19 The Daemon, Anthony Peake, Arcturus publishing Ltd 2008

P20 Of Two Minds, Frederic Schiffer MD, Simon and Schuster UK ltd 1999

P38 Zero Limits, Joe Vitale and Ihaleakala Hew Len, John Wiley and sons 2007

P58 The Law of Attraction, Esther and Jerry Hicks, Hay House UK Ltd 2006

P70 Autobiography of a Yogi, Paramahansa Yogananda, The Philosophical library 1946

P91/P174 The Philosophy Book Various, Dorling Kindersley Ltd 2011

P120 Consciousness beyond Life, Pim Van Lommel MD, Harper Collins 2010

P120 Reincarnation and Biology, Ian Pretyman Stevenson MD, Praeger Publishers 1997

P166 Why kindness is good for you, David R Hamilton PhD, Hay House UK Ltd 2010

P166 Pay it Forward Catherine Ryan, Hyde Barnes and Noble 1999

Films/Documentaries

P21 The Secret You, BBC Horizon, BBC, 2009

P32 The Matrix, The Wachowski Brothers, Warner Bros Pictures, 1999

P33 The Truman show, Andrew Niccol, Scott Rudin productions 1998

ABOUT THE AUTHOR

Theresa Borg BA (Hons) DHP DCH GQHP is the founder and director of Positively Joyous Hypnotherapy, Coaching and Meditation which is based in South East London. She has been a qualified Hypnotherapist since 2009 and completed her Psychotherapy diploma the following year. She has since built up a successful private practice based largely on word of mouth. Theresa is a Grade 1 'outstanding' teacher of positive psychology, spirituality, law of attraction and meditation courses. She is also a Reiki healer runs private spirituality, health and wellbeing courses throughout the UK.
Find out more about the book and Theresa's classes and courses at:

http://www.positivelyjoyous.com

DEDICATION

This book is dedicated to my wonderful son Steven. Thank you for your patience, help and support in getting this project off the ground. Thank you also to my loving family, the amazing teachers, students, clients and other authors who have helped me to build the knowledge and experience base that has made this book possible.

58331140R00120

Made in the USA
Charleston, SC
09 July 2016